DRESSAGE
An Introduction

DRESSAGE
An Introduction

Anthony Crossley

SWAN·HILL
PRESS

Copyright © 1992 by Executors of the late Anthony Crossley

First published in the UK in 1984 by Pelham Books Ltd.
This edition first published in 1992 by Swan Hill Press,
an imprint of Airlife Publishing Ltd.

British Library Cataloguing in Publication Data
A catalogue record is available for this book
from the British Library.

ISBN 1 85310 329 2

Printed by Livesey Limited, Shrewsbury.

Swan Hill Press

An imprint of Airlife Publishing Ltd.
101 Longden Road, Shrewsbury SY3 9EB.

Contents

Foreword

by Kalman de Jurenak

When one opens a book about riding, and particularly the art of dressage, I always first like to glance through the pictures and illustrations. If these are convincing and correspond to the true classical position of horse and rider, then I like to read the book.

Certainly that is the case with this wonderfully produced study by Anthony Crossley. Most impressive throughout is the clearness and simplicity with which he explains the true art of training, as well as giving an accurate picture of what dressage is all about without, as is so often unfortunately the case, confusing the reader with complicated and over technical explanations. It is in my opinion the best work on the subject that I have read in the English language.

Verden

Preface

Many books have been written about dressage, the great majority of them more or less directly concerned with giving advice to the reader on how he should ride and train his horse. I have indeed contributed to that library myself, with my two books: *Training the Young Horse, The First Two Years* and *Advanced Dressage*. Those were both, like their older and often famous companions, books primarily intended for immediate action by riders.

This book has a different purpose. It is intended to provide a comprehensive background against which, whether as rider or spectator, the reader can establish and develop his own appreciation and understanding of the history, purpose and philosophy of dressage within its classical concepts. Such understanding will also form the best possible basis for subsequent practical application on horseback. This book is in effect, and in the most literal sense of the word, a geography of dressage.

The two subjects dealt with in detail in the appendices at the end of the book, the Seat and the Half-halt, were first published as magazine articles (in *Riding*, 1982 and in *Horse & Driving*, 1983). Since they were well received in that context they have been reproduced here in their original form and consequently in somewhat greater detail than might have been appropriate as part of the main text of the book. They both rate very high in importance.

Many people in Great Britain still appear to find dressage riding a very mysterious affair and one which is therefore difficult to appreciate and to identify with. I hope this small book will help to guide them through the mysteries and into the daylight of understanding. I also hope that it will be of assistance, in the form of easily digestible but sound basic information, to riders who have perhaps only recently begun to study at first hand the practical aspects of this fascinating and lifelong pastime.

Training a dressage horse is a long and difficult process, full of subtle and intricate problems so numerous that they can never be fully explained on paper, though none of them can be overlooked or avoided by the serious practitioner. It can produce relatively fleeting moments of uplifting joy with, on even rarer occasions, an aesthetic element. It is more often concerned with the lengthy and arduous business of polishing basic skills and of developing the human virtues of patience, humility, sympathy, intelligence and self-discipline.

Anthony Crossley

Acknowledgements

When offering this book I am deeply indebted to Patricia Frost for the excellent line drawings with which she has complemented and embellished the text.

I also want to acknowledge my debt of gratitude to and admiration for the late Colonel Hans Handler whose deep understanding and clear explanations of the science and art of riding have long been a source of guidance to me, and on whose superb book, *The Spanish Riding School*, I have drawn for much assistance and information when writing my own.

1: History

Definition

The word 'dressage' derives from the French verb *dresser*, to set up, straighten up, train or break in (OED). Dressage therefore implies the processes or techniques involved in training, straightening up or breaking in, as applied to horses or, for that matter, any other animal. A *dresseur* can be translated as one who practises dressage. The universal use of the French word by English-speaking and other nations is explained by the fact that the dressage processes were most highly developed in modern times by the French, whose influence and writings have since spread around the world.

Antiquity

Humane, logical and systematic methods of training horses have their origins in very early history and were well established in the fifth century BC as part of the Greek culture and civilising influence. The earliest surviving literature on the subject are parts of two books written by the Greek historian, economist and philosopher Xenophon (430–354 BC) entitled *On the Art of Horsemanship* and *On the Cavalry Commander*. It is known that Xenophon spent almost the whole of his long life with horses and he is considered to be the founder of modern hippology, the science of horses and riding, although he himself acknowledges and quotes from an earlier work by an otherwise unknown person called Simon of Athens. Xenophon's own teaching remains entirely valid and serves as a model for the ethics of classical riding today. Even Simon of Athens apparently preached the highly civilised theory that 'a horse cannot be properly trained by whip and spur'.

Xenophon has left us many jewels of advice such as that 'the best rule and practice in dealing with a horse is never to approach him in anger', and that 'understanding and an approach to the animal's mentality are always preferable to brute force'.

It is probable that the general improvement of their cavalry, through the better manoeuvrability and reliability of their horses, formed the basis of Greek equestrian thought, but the work certainly included advanced training such as the piaffe and the levade, the latter being described by Xenophon in some detail.

Like many other aspects of Greek civilisation, those early and admirable principles of dressage training, that differ so little from what we understand and practise today, were lost or sadly neglected during the subsequent Roman and post-Roman periods. It was not until seventeen hundred years later, as part of the Italian Renaissance, that Xenophon's theories and methods were rediscovered and revived. The Romans appear to have been largely disinterested in riding as an art and then, in the so-called dark ages that followed the collapse of their Empire, life all over Europe became altogether too uncertain and barbaric for such sophistications to flourish.

Middle Ages

By the end of the tenth century AD the political shape of Europe was beginning to settle down after the five hundred years of invasions, migrations and counter-conquests that followed, and to a considerable extent expedited, the collapse of the Roman Empire. There began to be sufficient time and security for the development of some of the arts and entertainments that played an important part in the mediaeval Age of Chivalry, not least among them being the pageantry of Tournament Riding. Jousting, tilting and the mêlée, all of them competitive sports of some danger, encouraged the aristocracy and nobility to improve their horsemanship and required some basic training of their horses, though only for very simple movements and mostly at the walk and the gallop on straight lines. Written rules and regulations for Tournaments were in use by the year 1000.

There was little change from this rather crude use of the horse in war and warlike games until, in the fifteenth century and with the development of gunpowder and the use of small firearms by mounted men, it became vital, in order to survive in battle, to ride horses that were agile and manoeuvrable in all gaits and turns. These necessities, in conjunction with the contemporary rediscovery of the writings of antiquity, brought about a revival of the study and practice of classical horsemanship and horse-training, up to and including the use for battle purposes of the capriole.

Italian Renaissance: Sixteenth Century

The re-birth of the knowledge, skills and arts of classical Greece took place in Italy, and it was in Naples in 1532 that Frederico Grisone founded the first modern riding academy. Thither went the youth of noble families from all over Europe to learn the equestrian skills and manners that were by then considered to be required social graces for life at the courts of princes and kings. The importance of a good equestrian education for young aristocrats remained strong for three hundred years and was still in vogue when the young Arthur Wellesley, later the Duke of Wellington, was packed off to study at a school of equitation near Saumur when his progress at a famous English public school was not satisfying his parents.

Grisone had studied the written works of Xenophon, but from what we know from his own writings and about the bits he used, there can be little doubt that he employed unpleasantly forceful methods in breaking and training his horses.

Grisone's chief pupil and successor at Naples, and then at Rome, was Giovanni Pignatelli who is credited with being the inventor of the curb bit. A number of Pignatelli's pupils became outstanding riding-masters, setting up academies of their own in France, England, Austria and Denmark, and at the courts of many German princes. One of them, the Chevalier St Antoine, first taught the Neapolitan principles in England.

France: Seventeenth Century

The most notable and influential riding master in the early part of the seventeenth century was the Frenchman, Antoine Pluvinel de la Baume. A pupil of Giovanni Pignatelli, Pluvinel was closely connected with the royal court of Henry IV of France and opened a riding academy in Paris where he gave instruction to Henry's son, the future Louis XIII. In 1623 Pluvinel wrote *Le Manege Royal*, a beautifully illustrated work in the form of a dialogue between Louis and his teacher. Pluvinel's fame and importance in the annals of equestrian culture stem from his breakaway from the crude and often brutal methods of the Neapolitan School, setting new standards more in line with those advocated nearly two thousand years earlier by Xenophon. He tried to eliminate all rough treatment of horses and to achieve obedience through kindness and rewards.

England: Seventeenth Century

England's brief but spectacular moment of equestrian fame in the seventeenth century came when William Cavendish, companion in exile to Charles, Prince of

Wales (later to become King Charles II), opened a riding arena in Antwerp. In 1658, Cavendish published his now famous, and recently reprinted, book entitled *A General System of Horsemanship in All its Branches*. Returning to England at the restoration of the monarchy in 1660, Cavendish was made Duke of Newcastle in 1665.

Many subsequent writings by great masters have confirmed that Newcastle was a brilliant horseman who lived solely for his horses until he died at the age of eighty-four. Although he loved his horses and did not advocate harsh treatment, his failure to make a lasting impact on the development of dressage can be attributed to his willingness to use over-forceful methods and artificial aids such as the draw-rein which he is said to have invented. Nevertheless, he achieved much and his is one of the great names in the history of the art of riding.

France: Eighteenth Century

The greatest of all the post-Renaissance masters was François Robichon, Sieur de la Guerinière, a Frenchman very much of the same school of humane dressage as his earlier compatriot Pluvinel. Born in 1688, the son of a chamberlain to the Duke of Orleans, de la Guerinière first studied equitation in Paris under Françoise Anne de Vandeuil and, after ten years' wartime service as an officer, was awarded the title of Ecuyer Academiste which gave him the right to open his own school, which he did in 1717.

Guerinière's chief legacy to posterity lies in his book *Ecole de Cavalerie*, published in 1729. In it he completed the work begun by Pluvinel, effectively ostracising for ever the brutalities of the Neapolitans and the forceful shortcuts of Newcastle.

Ecole de Cavalerie contains virtually all that was known about dressage riding at that time including, at considerable length, the niceties of the movement called Shoulder-in, the invention of which is generally attributed to Guerinière. But much of what Guerinière speaks of was known by earlier masters and it is possible that the shoulder-in stems back to Newcastle's work. Steinbrecht, one of the great masters of the late nineteenth century, believed that to be the case.

Nevertheless, it was left to de la Guerinière to put together a thesis that embodied all the classic principles that revolutionised the art of riding throughout Europe by giving it a new, lasting and scientific foundation; and which provided a clear and precisely formulated system of training that has remained valid to this day and which still forms the basis of teaching at the Spanish Riding School in Vienna.

France: Nineteenth Century
After the collapse of the ancien régime and then, in 1815, of the Napoleonic Empire, the school of Versailles and of Guerinière had disappeared together with almost everybody who might have been able to pass on its skills and knowledge to a new era. Out of that void, a new school was set up at Saumur in 1814 for the benefit of cavalry training and, later on, for the development of civilian skills as well. Saumur, with its elite corps of instructors, the Cadre Noir, has survived to the present time, its peak period having been in the first forty years of this century during which the school produced many famous horsemen.

No account of French equitation in the nineteenth century is complete without mention of François Baucher and James Fillis. The former was widely acknowledged as a brilliant horseman and also as an ingenious and intelligent innovator of training techniques, more especially in the sphere of suppleness and obedience. His theories, however, contained some severe flaws which even he came to admit required revision.

James Fillis, an Englishman who went to France at an early age and worked there, in le Havre and Paris, for nearly forty years, came to be universally regarded as unquestionably the greatest rider in the world. He can fairly be called a genius, winning the highest respect from many great and important people for his extraordinary ability to produce, with the minimum apparent effort and time, impressive work from all kinds of horses. All his life he acknowledged his indebtedness to Baucher, though insisting on the need to modify the latter's weaknesses. Much of his work in France was, like that of Baucher, done in the circus, that being the only way in which it was possible for relatively impecunious people to show their horses to the public.

Fillis' success and prestige was such that, when at the age of sixty-three he visited Russia with the Circus Cineselli, he was immediately offered a ten-year commission as Colonel and Chief Ecuyer at the Imperial Russian Cavalry School, with responsibility for all riding instruction and the training of three hundred and fifty remount horses each year. This he is said to have accomplished without blemish to a single horse or serious accident to any rider. Fillis returned to Paris – still the metropolis of the equestrian world – in 1912, and died there in 1913.

Spain: Sixteenth Century

The history of the development of the art of riding in Spain, after the Italian renaissance, is shadowy although the two names of Vargas and Paolo d'Aquino survive. The wealth of the Spanish Imperial Court and the ready availability of the best horses in the world at that time make it certain that the subject was studied intensively. Pre-eminent among the riders was the founder of the Spanish Hapsburg dynasty, Charles 1 (1516–1556), whose reputation allowed William Cavendish, Duke of

Newcastle, to speak of him as having been 'unquestionably the best rider in his entire realm'.

In the long run, however, it was Austria that influenced the development of riding in Spain, rather than vice versa, through the connection of the two branches of the Hapsburg family. The term 'Spanish' used in connection with the great School in Vienna refers not to any style of riding developed in Spain, but solely to the origin of the type of horse used there. The Andalusian breeds were renowned throughout Europe as the best riding horses in the world, fit especially for kings and great men. Velasquez' portrait of Philip II, mounted on a typical high-quality Andalusian, now hangs in the National Gallery in London, while just outside stands le Sieur's bronze statue of Charles I on a fine horse of clearly the same breed.

Austria and the Spanish School in Vienna

At the end of the middle ages, Austria was an archdukedom of little more political importance than any of the other German states that comprised that area of central Europe later to be known as Germany. However, Vienna then became the heart of the Holy Roman Empire and also, by the eighteenth century, the capital of the Austro-Hungarian empire. In the former capacity alone its rulers had powerful links with the whole or most of Europe, especially with Italy, Spain, England, the Netherlands and France. It was consequently not just a matter of chance that the Imperial Court should gradually assume, after the collapse of the ancien régime in France, the mantle of protector of the classical art of riding.

The Emperor Maximilian II (1564–1576) imported Spanish-bred (Andalusian) horses for use in his court riding school in Vienna, and it was in his reign, in 1572, that the first documentary reference to the construction of a new 'Spanish Riding Hall' occurs, ie a hall or arena where the Spanish horses would be worked. In 1580 the Archduke Charles II, brother of Emperor Maximilian II, founded a breeding stud for the Spanish horses at Lippiza, near Trieste, which was then part of the domains of the Austrian Hapsburgs. It was at Lippiza that, as another document tells us, 'the best horses are bred for the use of the Imperial Court'. The fame of that district, with its large areas of rock and very sparse vegetation, for breeding horses goes back to Roman times. The Spanish or Andalusian strain of Lippizaner horse used in Vienna was at later dates reinforced by the deliberate introduction of German, Italian, Danish and pure Arab blood.

Lippiza remained the home of the Imperial stud, in the process giving its name to the horses bred there, until the breakup of the Austro-Hungarian empire at the end of World War 1 when, in 1920, some of the animals went to Hungary to form the Budapest Spanish Riding School. The remainder were divided between the new Republic of Austria, the new state of Yugoslavia and Italy, in whose territory Lippiza then fell. The Austrian stud was re-established at Piber in Styria where it still flourishes today.

Now, in the latter half of the twentieth century, the Spanish School in Vienna stands alone as the pre-eminent if not the only academy dedicated solely to the preservation of the classical art of riding.

Its influence throughout the world, with special regard to the humanitarian methods of training, has been and remains immense. A few names stand out among the many who have helped to establish and maintain its now traditional standards, foremost among them being the family of Weyrother, four members of which rose in the service of the school to the rank of Chief Rider: Adam von Weyrother (1729–40); Franz von Weyrother (1754–

60); Gottlieb von Weyrother (1810–28); and, of exceptional importance to the development of the school dogma, Maximilian von Weyrother (1813–33). It was the latter member of this illustrious family who imported and adapted to the Vienna School methods, the teachings of François Robichon de la Guerinière, thereby confirming the permanent influence, to this day, of the great French Master.

Max von Weyrother's two books, *Determining the Proper Bit and Bridle* (1814) and the posthumous *Fragments and Unpublished Writings* (1836), followed Guerinière meticulously and have been especially influential, together with the writings of Seeger, Oyenhausen and Field Marshal Franz Holbein von Holbeinsberg (*Directives for the Implementation of a Methodical Procedure for the Training of Riders and Horses at the Imperial Spanish Riding School*, 1898) in setting an authoritative standard for classical dressage riding and training as it is known today. It is a doctrine built on and around humanity, logic, method and patience.

The science and art of classical riding was developed in antiquity, rediscovered in Italy, advanced in Spain, England and Germany, and came to its fullest flowering in France. It is practised today, solely for its own sake and for the great benefit of posterity, at the Spanish Riding School in Vienna.

Germany: Sixteenth Century
Until the second half of the nineteenth century, Germany comprised a large number of independent kingdoms, dukedoms and principalities, chief among them being Prussia, Hannover, Bavaria, Oldenburg, Saxony, Brunswick, Brandenburg and the Palatinate. Each had its own court life, and at most of the courts a degree of proficiency at school-riding and haute école was regarded as a status-giving accomplishment.

In the seventeenth century only the name of George Engelhard von Löhneyssen is notable as having carried the Italian teaching to Brunswick, where he worked as court equerry and where he wrote, in 1588, a book on bits and bitting. The esteem in which Spanish horses were held, even at that time, throughout Europe is evidenced in a later edition of his book in which he said 'of all the horses on earth, the Spaniards are the most intelligent, the most likeable and the most gentle'.

Germany: Nineteenth Century

In the nineteenth century the names of Louis Seeger, von Oyenhausen and Gustav Steinbrecht are pre-eminent among many famous exponents of the art of riding then practising and teaching in the German states. Seeger's book, *A System for the Art of Riding*, published in 1884 and clearly influenced by the great Maximilian von Weyrother (see Austria, page 20) under whom Seeger had studied in Vienna, was considered to be the standard work of that period. Von Oyenhausen, also a student of the Spanish Riding School, published in 1848 *A Guide to the Finishing of Horse and Rider*. Steinbrecht's book, *The Gymnasium of the Horse*, published in 1885, is probably the greatest book after Guerinière's *Ecole de Cavalerie* and is a classic of great value today though unfortunately not yet available in the English language.

The World: Twentieth Century

For the past two and a half thousand years, dressage training has been studied and practised mainly for the greater efficiency of cavalry in war; for the encouragement of courtly manners and education; for entertainment and display; and for its sheer artistic merit. But in the last half of the twentieth century it has become more and more firmly regarded and practised as a sport in its own right and in the form of national and international competitions. It has become increasingly rare to find riders who are prepared to eschew the challenge and the stimulus of the competition arena and to devote their lives to the study of dressage as a science and an art. The names of Nuno Oliveira (Portugal) and Egon von Neindorf (Germany) stand out among those who have done so.

This comparatively recent introduction of the competitive element has its advantages and its disadvantages. It can be said to assist in preserving the vitality of academic riding through being performed in public and in front of judges, and competition alone has justified the establishment for the first time of internationally accepted written rules for classical dressage. On the other hand, competition inevitably brings with it an element of pressure that can all too easily lead to hurried methods, shortcuts and the sacrifice of principle in favour of expediency, the wish to win taking precedence over the desire to study. However, this era of competition has undoubtedly broadened the public interest in the intellectual aspects of riding, to the great benefit of riding itself and of the horses that are ridden.

Discussion is often heard on the question of whether dressage riding is basically an art or a craft. It was wisely said by Colonel Hans Handler, who died in the saddle and in the service of the Spanish Riding School in 1972, that classical riding is a matter of both a science and an art, the latter being developed from the former in so far as the two parties are together capable of it. Every dressage rider has the opportunity to be an artist. Colonel Handler added that the result of classical dressage is a work of art, though not necessarily of good art, depending on the degree of harmony and movement attained.

International Dressage: Twentieth Century
Outside the citadel of the Spanish Riding School,

dressage in the twentieth century – and more especially in the latter half of the century – has been wholly dominated by international competition and is hardly recognised in any other sphere of equestrian activity. A very few circuses continue to show skilful and even pure work, notably that of Frederick Knee of Switzerland. A few displays are given from time to time as part of some other form of public entertainment, but these are usually performed by riders who have become famous as a result of success in competition. Nevertheless, good quality displays are always popular, even with relatively un-informed audiences, presumably for their artistic merit. On the other hand (and paradoxically) competition dressage, except at the highest level or on the most prestigious occasion, will seldom attract a really big audience, presumably because the spectacle tends to appear repetitious and somewhat long-drawn-out.

The proficiency of the various nations participating in international dressage has varied over the years and would appear to have been conditioned largely by historical, geographical and climatic factors. For example, the difficult winter climate of Eastern and Central Europe, combined with the sustained interest in haute école in the numerous royal or ducal courts, did much to establish a wide interest in indoor riding in those regions; whereas the popularity and climatic availability of the fascinating and exciting sport of foxhunting, ever since its development in the early eighteenth century, has almost entirely absorbed equestrian enthusiasms in England. Hence our neglect and comparative ignorance of dressage riding. Nations whose continuity and stability of life have not been shaken by the impact of great wars (eg Sweden) have also benefited.

The present widespread growth of competitive dress-age, both national and international, can be said to date from 1912 when dressage was first included in the

Olympic Games, at Stockholm. Since then, and up to
1988, there has been a total of seventeen Olympic
Games, the results of which can be used as a guide to
the understanding and proficiency in dressage among
the leading equestrian nations of the world. Taking
only the winning of team or individual Olympic medals
as a yardstick, the following figures emerge:

OLYMPIC MEDALS

1912–1988: 17 Olympic Games

Sweden	22 medals	12 Individual	(5 Gold)	
		10 Team	(5 Gold) Overall 10 Gold	
Germany	30 medals	17 Individual	(4 Gold)	
		13 Team	(7 Gold) Overall 15 Gold	
France	13 medals	7 Individual	(1 Gold)	
		6 Team	(2 Gold) Overall 3 Gold	
Switzerland	17 medals	8 Individual	(4 Gold)	
		9 Team	(0 Gold) Overall 4 Gold	
USSR	6 medals	4 Individual	(2 Gold)	
		2 Team	(1 Gold) Overall 3 Gold	
USA	5 medals	1 Individual	(0 Gold)	
		4 Team	(0 Gold) Overall 0 Gold	
Denmark	5 medals	4 Individual	(0 Gold)	
		1 Team	(0 Gold) Overall 0 Gold	
Austria	1 medal	1 Individual	(0 Gold) Overall 0 Gold	
Holland	1 medal	1 Team	(0 Gold) Overall 0 Gold	
Czechoslovakia	1 medal	1 Team	(0 Gold) Overall 0 Gold	
Portugal	1 medal	1 Team	(0 Gold) Overall 0 Gold	
Canada	1 medal	1 Team	(0 Gold) Overall 0 Gold	

Notes

(1) Great Britain has never yet won an Olympic dressage medal.

(2) Sweden's main successes were scored in the three Olympics between 1912 and 1924, during which period they won all the Gold medals, and all the Individual medals except one Bronze. These achievements emanated from the high standard of their cavalry school at Stromsholm and their neutrality during the 1914–18 war.

(3) France's ascendency, based on the cavalry school and Cadre Noir at Saumur, followed that of Sweden in the short period 1928–32.

(4) Germany took a brief lead at the Berlin Games in 1936, but did not score again, as a result of her total defeat in the 1939–45 war, until 1956 when, at Helsinki, her riders won the Individual Bronze and a team Silver. In each of the last nine Games, 1956–1988, Germany has won at least one of the Individual medals; and in the last seven Games the German Team has been beaten into second place only once, by the USSR in 1972.

(5) Switzerland's medals, all taken after 1948, were mainly founded on her Cavalry School and, after the school closed, on one exceptionally brilliant horse, Granat, ridden by Christine Stückelberger.

(6) The USSR won their first medal in 1960 and their last in 1972.

(7) In compiling the data quoted above, the 1980 Games have been taken to be the Alternative Games held at Goodwood (GB) rather than the official venue of Moscow where few nations took part.

OLYMPIC RESULTS

INDIVIDUAL DRESSAGE

	1 (Gold)	2 (Silver)	3 (Bronze)	Teams
1912 STOCKHOLM	Sweden EMPEROR (Bonde)	Sweden NEPTUNE (Boltenstern)	Sweden MAGGIE (Blixen-Finecke)	1. Sweden 2. Germany 3. France
1920 ANTWERP	Sweden UNO (Lundblad)	Sweden SABEL (Sandstrom)	Sweden RUNNING SISTER (von Rosen)	1. Sweden 2. France 3. USA
1924 PARIS	Sweden PICCOLOMINI (Linder)	Sweden SABEL (Sandstrom)	France PLUNARD (Lesage)	1. Sweden 2. France 3. Czechoslovakia
1928 AMSTERDAM	Germany DRAUFGÄNGER (von Langen)	France LINON (Marion)	Sweden GUNSTLING (Olson)	1. Germany 2. Sweden 3. Holland
1932 LOS ANGELES	France TAINE (Lesage)	France LINON (Marion)	USA OLYMPIC (Tuttle)	1. France 2. Sweden 3. USA
1936 BERLIN	Germany KRONOS (Pollay)	Germany ABSINTH (Gerhard)	Austria NERO (Podhajsky)	1. Germany 2. France 3. Sweden
1948 LONDON	Switzerland HUMMER (Moser)	France HARPAGON (Jousseaume)	Sweden TRUMF (Boltenstern)	1. France 2. USA 3. Portugal
1952 HELSINKI	Sweden MASTER RUFUS (St Cyr)	Denmark JUBILEE (Hartel)	France HARPAGON (Jousseaume)	1. Sweden 2. Switzerland 3. Germany
1956 STOCKHOLM	Sweden JULI XX (St Cyr)	Denmark JUBILEE (Hartel)	Germany ADULAR (Linsenhoff)	1. Sweden 2. Germany 3. Switzerland
1960 ROME	USSR ABSENT (Filatov)	Switzerland WALD (Fischer)	Germany ASBACH (Neckermann)	No team awards
1964 TOKYO	Switzerland WOERMANN (Chammartin)	Germany REMUS (Boldt)	USSR ABSENT (Filatov)	1. Germany 2. Switzerland 3. Russia
1968 MEXICO	USSR IKHOR (Kizimov)	Germany MARIANO (Neckermann)	Germany DUX (Kimke)	1. Germany 2. USSR 3. Switzerland

	1 (Gold)	2 (Silver)	3 (Bronze)	Teams
1972 MUNICH	Germany PIAFF (Lisenhoff)	USSR PEPEL (Petuchkova)	Germany VENETIA (Neckermann)	1. USSR 2. Germany 3. Sweden
1976 MONTREAL	Switzerland GRANAT (Stüeckelberger)	Germany WOYCEK (Boldt)	Germany MEHMED (Klimke)	1. Germany 2. Switzerland 3. USA
1980 GOODWOOD (Alternative Olympics)	Switzerland GRANAT (Stüeckelberger)	Germany SLIVOWITZ (Schulten-Baumer)	Germany AHLERICH (Klimke)	1. Germany 2. Switzerland 3. Denmark
1984 LOS ANGELES	Germany AHLERICH (Klimke)	Denmark MARZOG (Jensen)	Switzerland LIMANDUS (Hoffer)	1. Germany 2. Switzerland 3. Sweden
1988 SEOUL	Germany REMBRANDT 24 (Uphoff)	France CORLANDUS (Otto-Crepin)	Switzerland GAUGIN DE LULLY (Stüeckelberger)	1. Germany 2. France 3. Canada

2: The Dressage Horse

There is, strictly speaking, no such thing as a dressage type of horse. As with hunters, showjumpers, racehorses and polo-ponies, they come in all shapes and sizes. What is wanted for dressage, and for virtually all the other equestrian activities, is simply a good horse; that is to say, a horse of sound conformation that will consequently, in all probability, stand up to work for many years. Dressage training, if taken up to the high school, will

Fig. 1 *A good horse. Well positioned and well let down hocks; neck well set on at withers; strong loins; good shoulder; small head, powerful quarters; open gullet; feet and pasterns at same angle with moderate slope.*

impose great strain on the horse's physique, especially on the back, loins and hindquarters. There is also an element of elegance to be considered and so, although this need not involve the matter of beauty and good looks, it does mean that overall symmetry, proportion and correct natural movement of all four limbs should be considered. A thoroughly cooperative temperament is of particular importance because any inherent and deep-set lack of obedience can very easily, in the long run, destroy the whole project. The horse, like the rider, requires temperamental patience and stamina.

It is clear that this short outline of what to look for in a horse that is destined to be trained for the high school of dressage conforms entirely with the age-old description, written about in many books by the most experienced

Fig. 2 *A poor horse. Poorly positioned and weak hocks; neck set on too low; weak loins; poor, straight shoulder; upright pasterns; disproportionately long legs; body lacking depth.*

horsemen, of what a good horse should look like. Within those prescribed limits, the more perfect the conformation the more suitable the animal is likely to be for dressage, or for hunting, or for steeplechasing, or for showjumping, or for virtually any other strenuous physical activity. A person who is 'a good judge of a horse' will, even if he knows nothing about dressage, quite easily pick out a good dressage horse. A good horse is a good horse, for whatever purpose.

But of course no horse yet born has been *entirely* perfect in all aspects of his conformation. There has been, and always will be, some weakness here or there; some aspect that is more open to criticism than others. It becomes a question of trying to select for dressage a horse with as few disadvantageous, and as many advantageous, aspects of his make and shape as possible; not forgetting, in so far as is practicable, the animal's temperament and internal organs.

Special Requirements

The accepted good points of the ideal horse are beyond dispute and well documented. But because of the impossibility of finding such a paragon, it may be helpful to list just a few of the weaknesses that the prospective buyer of a dressage horse should take particular care to avoid.

(1) The hindlegs should by nature fall down from the hips in such a manner that the hocks are readily available to carry out their dual role of creating forward impulsion and carrying, for long periods, a greater than usual proportion of the total weight of the horse. If they tend to fall out behind under normal conditions, they will be that much more difficult to engage further forward when a high degree of collection is called for, as it must frequently be in serious dressage. It is obviously better to have them well and handily placed in the first instance.

(2) The ability of a horse to engage his hind-legs further under the mass, in order to lighten his forehand, will depend very much on his ability to flex his hocks in his ordinary and free paces. This can be judged by watching the horse moving on a lunge rein or even free in a field. If the hock-joints appear stiff and unbending, it does not bode well for the ultimate attainment of collection.

(3) It is the trainer's purpose and business to develop and improve the horse's natural movement and paces. Quite normal paces are therefore a satisfactory basis for that process which aims at increasing collection as well as extension, both of them in easy, flowing rhythm. It is not at all necessary, and can even be a disadvantage, to have a horse whose normal paces, especially in walk or trot, are in any way exaggerated or, as it is often said, extravagant. So long as they are free, loose and unconstrained, progress should not be difficult. The rest is up to the skill of the rider.

(4) It is very unwise to think that, if a horse is chicken-hearted or constitutionally unfitted for some other robust equestrian sport, he may be good enough for dressage.

(5) The loin, just in front of the croup, should be level, not dipped, so it will not be difficult to develop the muscles to execute the heavy work of lifting the forehand.

(6) The neck should be well set on and flow smoothly out of the withers. This again will facilitate the lifting and lightening of the forehand.

(7) The head should not appear disproportionately big (heavy) as that would be a tiring burden for the horse at the end of its neck. There should be plenty of room between the cheek-bones and through the gullet, for comfortable and easy flexion at the poll.

(8) The slope of the pasterns should be neither too steep nor too low. The former will tend to jar the horse and will certainly make him uncomfortable to sit on. The latter

will impose too much strain on the tendons, especially in extensions and in the elevated paces of piaffe and, still more, passage.

(9) Results indicate the difficulty, or even impossibility of selecting any one type or breed of horse as being more likely to be successful in dressage competition than the rest. International success, at Olympic, World or European championship level, has been achieved by thoroughbred or thoroughbred-type horses; by horses carefully bred with dressage in mind, such as the German and Swedish breeds; by small, crossbred horses such as the 15.1½ hh Connemara x TB Little Model (GB) or the little black Russian stallion Pepel; or by the rather coarse, essentially inelegant (except when in movement) but phenomenal dressage horse, the Holsteiner Granat; and by the huge, powerful, broad, and again not very elegant, Hanoverian Woyceck. These, and many others, have made great names for themselves but have each been unique and unlike any other on the roll of honour. There is no recognisable average. The key to great success lies mainly in the rider, aided by the inherent and natural flair of the horse, provided only that it is conformationally and constitutionally a good horse.

3: The Dressage Rider

Responsibilities

The rider who undertakes to train a dressage horse becomes directly and wholly responsible for the development of the character as well as the physical abilities of his pupil. If he does not do the job well, the horse will be spoilt, to a greater or lesser extent, for the rest of his life. The training process, if completed, will take many years and, by the end of that time, any faults of character or manner of performance created by poor training techniques will have become so firmly entrenched that they will be extremely difficult, or even impossible, to eradicate. Further, the rider must accept as beyond dispute that he, not the horse, will always be responsible for all training faults that occur. If the pupil hasn't learnt, the teacher hasn't taught. Conversely, if the horse learns or acquires a bad habit, it has to be the rider who has taught or allowed it. To blame the horse for anything is the negation of the basic principles of dressage training.

It must be assumed that no horse has any wish or even the ability to learn any new thing by or for himself, or to make any improvement in his natural and instinctive manner of movement or behaviour. He will display no initiative in either case and will only learn by the process of being taught. Everything therefore depends on the knowledge and the teaching ability of the rider. He alone will carry the credit or the blame for the final result.

It follows that the rider must ensure that he knows precisely what he wants to teach and precisely how it can or should be taught. And since the teaching is mainly done from the saddle, he must in addition be a very good rider so that his own physical inefficiencies and fumblings do not blur the lesson he is trying to teach. Thus we have to face the fact that no horse can learn anything well unless his rider can ride well and teach well. In short, no horse can be better than his rider. If the horse fails, it will always be the fault of the rider. It is never the horse's fault.

These things amount to awesome responsibilities for the dressage rider, responsibilities to which he must constantly give much thought and study. He should regard each and every shortcoming in respect of his knowledge of his subject – his riding ability; his patience or temper; his failure to plan his teaching programme methodically and systematically – as a shame on himself and an insult to his horse. He must set and maintain for himself the highest standards of efficiency and behaviour. His horse will assuredly then follow in his steps.

Styles

There is only one style of dressage riding of any importance and that is the classical style – or what has come to be known over the last four hundred years, as the classical style. The main requirements of this style are those of balance and harmony. The rider must be able to ride on and in harmony with his horse by balance alone, so that there will never be any form of grip or muscular contraction except for the specific purpose of communicating a precise and limited message. His balance must be such that he can follow all the movements his horse may make, whether anticipated or not, without losing that balance and without resort to gripping with legs or hands, since that would jeopardise his ability to communicate sensitively and put him out of harmony.

To achieve this degree of balance, the rider must sit with all the parts of his body, the bones of his pelvis, spine, shoulders and head, poised and balanced one above the other in a vertical plane, each part balanced on and supported by the one below, so that no muscular tension is required to hold them together and prevent them from falling apart. To achieve this he will dispose his body in exactly the same position as a well-behaved person would adopt at a formal dinner party at which there are no backs to the chairs. And the key to that balanced posture lies in the positioning of the pelvis, which forms the base of the whole structure. It is necessary to rock or tilt the top of the pelvis somewhat forward of the position it tends to adopt of its own accord or when a person is sitting in a slovenly manner. The forward tilt of the upper part only of the pelvis places it under the rib-cage and directly over the seat-bones which will then, as indeed they must, carry the whole weight of the torso (see Fig. 3). It is a position in which the rider is alert and ready for anything.

In addition to being efficiently balanced, the rider requires to be both supple and relaxed, but without allowing the relaxation to affect his poised balance and alertness. In particular he must be supple in the region of his loin or lower spine in order to enable him to absorb the bumping, the up-and-down movement, that is an inevitable factor in a moving horse. A satisfactory blend of balance and suppleness is always recognisable by the fact that the rider appears then to be entirely unmoved or disturbed by the most active paces and movements; whereas the unbalanced or stiff rider will be seen to bump in the saddle with every stride and to have inelegant and tiresome movement in the upper part of the torso and in his head. That disturbance is, in the long term, injurious to both rider and horse and, even in the short term, extremely uncomfortable for the horse.

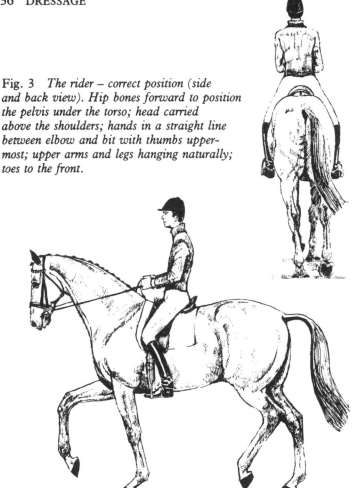

Fig. 3 *The rider – correct position (side and back view). Hip bones forward to position the pelvis under the torso; head carried above the shoulders; hands in a straight line between elbow and bit with thumbs uppermost; upper arms and legs hanging naturally; toes to the front.*

In order to be relaxed or, in other words, free from any muscular contraction, it is not enough that the different parts of the torso should be poised, one above the other, in perfect balance over the seat-bones. The rider must also:

(a) Allow his legs to hang down in the perfectly natural position imposed on them by their own gravitational weight. The knee must not be drawn upwards and the lower-leg will hang slightly behind the vertical to counterbalance the weight of the foot on the front of it. The leg will quite automatically hang in that position provided the rider does not make any conscious muscular effort to draw it further back or to thrust it further forward. It should remain perfectly still at all times, lying close to the horse near the girth, unless it is specifically required to move it back a little to give a controlling aid or message to the quarters.

(b) Allow his shoulders and upper arms to hang down vertically, by gravity, with the elbows lightly brushing his sides, and with no stiffening or muscular contraction in the shoulder or elbow joints.

(c) Allow the rein contact with the horse's mouth to draw his forearms, wrists and hands into a straight line, when viewed from the side, between the elbow, hand and bit. For this purpose, the hands should be held with their backs in line with the forearm and with the thumbs uppermost. That is the position into which the hands fall naturally when wholly relaxed; the position in which they are most sensitive; and the position in which they can operate with the greatest sympathy and delicacy in conjunction with the horse's mouth.

Every rider must inevitably impose some inconvenience on his horse by the mere fact of his being in the saddle. But if he has trained himself to conform meticulously and continuously to these basic rules of good riding, that inconvenience will be reduced to the minimum and he will have gone a very long way towards obtaining the best that his horse is capable of giving.

The subject of the rider's seat is discussed in greater detail in Appendix A, page 153.

Rider's Aids
The means by which the rider communicates with,

instructs, or causes his horse to function in some specific manner are called The Aids. These comprise Leg Aids, Rein Aids, and Seat Aids. In addition there are various auxiliary aids, namely the whip, the spur, the voice and the caress.

Leg Aids   The prime purpose of leg aids is to stimulate the horse to go forward with activity and impulsion. Their subsidiary purposes are to control the hindquarters; to create lateral or sideways movement when required; and to assist in suppling the horse by forming a pivot round which the forward portion of the horse's spine can be bent, eg when he is moving on a circle or a curved track.

The prime purpose of creating forward activity is achieved by a pressure of both legs acting inwards and very slightly forwards, the latter aspect being so slight that it is virtually invisible to an observer. A purely inward pressure has very little logic or meaning for a horse, and the crude or 'old-fashioned' backward pressure or kick is totally illogical and if fully implemented can only result in hurting the horse with the spur, which is unethical in any case.

When used for the secondary purpose of actively producing, or more passively prohibiting, lateral movement of the whole horse or of the hindquarters alone, the relevant leg should be moved only slightly back behind its normal position on the girth, perhaps about one inch for the former task and not more than about three inches for the latter. But even while being used in this manner, the leg will still have to play its part, in conjunction with the other leg, in maintaining forward impulsion. This becomes progressively difficult, and ultimately impossible, as the legs get further back behind the girth.

The Spur   The use of the spur, which is one aspect of a

leg aid, should be a rare occurrence. When it is necessary to bring the spur into use it should be done in such a way that it merely reinforces, but does not contradict, the forward element of the normal leg pressure. This is achieved by simply turning out the toe a little as the leg acts inward and forward, so that the heel comes closer to the horse and the spur makes contact with the skin while being drawn forward against the lie of the hair in a relatively gentle manner. The spur thus retains all the logic of the basic leg aid and does not harm or alarm the horse.

The spur should be regarded and used only as an ultimate sanction, or as an implied threat. It must be the rider's aim to train his horse from the beginning to respond to and obey promptly the quiet but positive muscular pressure of the inside of the leg in whatever position it is applied. Only if that fails, or the horse has become lazy, should the leg pressure be followed by the spur contact.

Rein Aids The purpose of aids given by the reins is to control and direct the impulsive energy from the quarters already created by the leg aids. The rider's hands, through the reins, should achieve these purposes by either yielding, restraining or opposing. Never, even when opposing, should the hands pull backwards, as this contradicts and tends to destroy the life-enhancing forward impulsion.

The greater the skill of the rider and the higher the state of training of the horse, the more the rein aids tend to take over, from the legs, the control of direction in lateral movements, thus allowing the legs to be increasingly concerned with and concentrated on the creation and maintenance of impulsion.

The directional use of the rein aids, at all stages of training, is achieved by the employment of judicious variations of the infinite number of angles and pressures available to the rider. For the sake of simplicity, the many possible variations of rein aids are normally reduced to five and are referred to as the Five Rein Effects. They each have an automatic and quite inescapable mechanical influence on the direction of movement of the main portions of the horse's body. (See Fig. 4.) The use of any one of these rein effects must, unless the horse positively resists, cause him to move in the manner or direction indicated in the diagram. In practice, combinations of any two of the five effects will almost always be used to achieve the rider's purpose.

The five basic rein effects are:

(1)   the direct, or open, rein;
(2)   the indirect rein;
(3)   the direct rein of opposition;
(4)   the indirect rein of opposition in front of the withers;
(5)   the indirect rein of opposition behind the withers.

Since the very great majority of riders are somewhat less than perfect in their ability to control their seat and, consequently, their hands – and since they are therefore likely, if unwittingly, to use their reins from time to time in a manner that they do not intend – it becomes important that these basic and not very complicated rein effects should be thoroughly understood and mastered from the outset of a dressage rider's career. See Fig. 4.

Seat Aids   The seat aids comprise the influence of the weight of the rider on one or both of his seat-bones combined with and modified by appropriate action of the muscles of the loins. They are very closely allied to leg aids and are used primarily to assist the legs in driving or urging the horse forward or, occasionally, in a less mobile manner, to restrict the impulsion as it passes through the

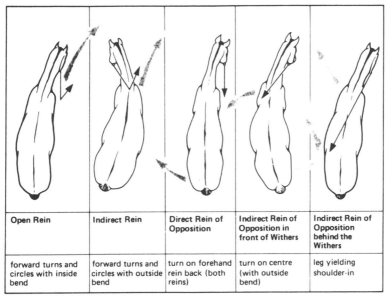

Open Rein	Indirect Rein	Direct Rein of Opposition	Indirect Rein of Opposition in front of Withers	Indirect Rein of Opposition behind the Withers
forward turns and circles with inside bend	forward turns and circles with outside bend	turn on forehand rein back (both reins)	turn on centre (with outside bend)	leg yielding shoulder-in

Note: small arrow indicates direction of rein effect
large arrow indicates direction of consequent movement of the horse

Fig. 4   *The rein effects.*

swinging back of the horse.

The rider's seat, that is to say his weight on his seat-bones in the saddle, can be passive as when there is no positive muscular action of the loins; or active, as when there is positive and deliberate muscular action. The muscular action, usually called 'bracing the back', has the momentary effect of decreasing the natural suppleness of the rider's lumbar spine and thereby proportionately increasing, in the forward direction, the pressure of the weight on one or both seat-bones, depending on whether the muscular action is unilateral or bilateral, ie whether one or both sides of the loin is brought into play. This will be determined by the precise result the rider wishes to obtain. In either case, the seat-bone(s) will be pressed more or less strongly downwards and forwards into the saddle, without actually moving it (them) along the surface of the saddle, and usually in coordination with a complementary use of the legs.

Weight (or seat) aids, whether driving or restraining, can only be effective on a back that has been strengthened, is relaxed and is swinging. A horse's back can be swinging only when the horse is in motion and it follows that weight aids can have no effect, and indeed have no meaning, on a stationary horse.

No single aid should ever be used in isolation. The desired effect on a horse must only, but always, be achieved by the combined use of all the aids, the legs, the hands and the seat, when the horse is in motion or is just becoming mobile, although any one of these may predominate over the others.

When the horse understands how to respond to the stimuli of the legs, hands and seat, and when he is physically ready and mentally willing to comply, he is said to be 'on the aids', or to have been 'put to the aids'.

With a well-schooled horse and a skilful rider, the aids can be so refined that the rider will hardly do more than think what he wishes to do and the horse will respond in perfect harmony.

4: Training Principles

Age of Horse

No rider who has the long-term development of his horse at heart will attempt to ride, or even to lunge, a young horse until he is three years old. Before that time the animal's bones are not sufficiently set and are consequently unlikely to be able to take the strain that would be imposed on them without grave risk of immediate or long-term damage. The fact that this precept is seldom followed in the world of racing does nothing to invalidate it. Maybe the conditions and requirements of the youngster there will be different in so far as the jockeys have the weight of small children and the animals do virtually all their work on straight lines; but the main and saddest factor is the commercial one, and the fact that, with exceedingly few exceptions, the animal's growth and development into middle or old age is of practically no interest. Young flat-racehorses are programmed to function as best they can for two or three years only, beginning at the age of two. Of those that survive, a few may be worth a lot of money, but the majority are relegated to oblivion, broken in health or character.

It is true that some of those that have survived the fairly crude rigours of their youthful education in a racing stable have gone on, in good hands, to become very well-trained dressage horses, and that is more than can be said for youngsters trained in their early days for the show-ring. The success of the ex-racehorse in dressage is no doubt explained by the fact that they are all ridden in the early days exclusively in a simple snaffle bridle and are asked only to go forwards. Their mouths and their balance, though not by any means carefully developed, are seldom irretrievably spoilt.

It is quite reasonable to begin the dressage training of a horse, assuming it to have been previously unbroken or backed, at any time up to the age of five or six. If, on the other hand, it has already been sensibly handled, backed and worked in some other sphere of sport, and has not been spoilt in the process, then seven or even eight years would not be unreasonable for a start in dressage, although hardly ideal. A great deal depends on just how high up the dressage ladder the trainer is aiming with that particular horse. Dressage is not, or need not be, entirely a matter of Grand Prix competitions. But the top level does take many years to reach and, bearing in mind all the troubles, problems and set-backs that can occur along the route, not to mention the time and the money involved, it is hardly advisable to undertake the task with a horse that will probably be going downhill by the time it is completed, leaving no time for the trainer to enjoy the final results of his labours.

A serious dressage rider will prefer to buy a new horse at the age of three or four, preferably before; but failing that, just after it has been backed. He will then be in a position to accept full responsibility for the whole of the horse's education and will not be purchasing other men's mistakes. The time required to complete that education, equivalent perhaps to a university honours degree course, or full Grand Prix standard dressage, will depend particularly on the experience and talent of the trainer and also, though to a somewhat lesser extent, on the intelligence and natural talent of the horse. Given an apt pupil with really good athletic ability and a bright, cooperative temperament, the very experienced trainer may produce a reasonably well finished and polished horse in four or five years, the horse then being seven or eight years old. Thereafter, if the work has been well done, the horse will continue to show further improvement and polish for perhaps another eight years. But then, at about fifteen or sixteen years of age, or perhaps a little earlier, he will almost certainly have reached his peak and be showing signs of old age and loss of gymnastic ability. Even then however, if the development has been steady and unforced, and he has been fortunate in his health, he may reach his third decade and still be enjoying with his proud rider a happy and active life. In the World Championships of 1982, a Holsteiner gelding calling Granat, owned, trained and ridden by Christine Stückelberger of Switzerland, was only narrowly beaten for the Gold medal, at the age of seventeen.

Achievement
The optimum figures just suggested may perhaps be exceptional. If the initial training work is rushed and compressed still further there will be a grave risk, amounting to a probability, that the pressure will be too great for the horse's mental or physical welfare; breakdown of one sort or another will sooner or later occur; the training results will be flawed; and the horse will not remain a pleasure to himself or to his rider into a ripe old age. Conversely, riders with too little or no previous experience of training a dressage horse may take ten or even more years to reach a respectable Grand Prix standard from a three-year-old start, leaving only a year or so in hand.

The length of time needed to build up and develop a dressage horse to his full potential can be kept in perspective by comparison with the time taken to do the same for a human athlete, gymnast, dancer or golfer. All of them require many years of training, both mind and body. By contrast, the task with a horse is made the more difficult by the fact that he is much larger and heavier; is inarticulate; is not particularly intelligent; and is expected to carry an unnatural load on his back.

Stages of Training

Although the training of a horse comprises one continuous process of steady and gradual development, without any clear-cut breaks but depending for its length on the ultimate standard aimed at, it is convenient to consider the work as being divided into stages. These stages provide opportunities to assess progress and make such adjustments as may seem appropriate.

Details of any training programme and its stages are bound to vary as between one trainer and another, according to their individual opinions, experience and knowledge. Nevertheless, equestrian experience over the last five hundred years has helped to establish what may be called a classical progression for training horses to the highest flights and that progression is most clearly set out in the staged work-schedule advocated and followed by the Spanish Riding School in Vienna. It is today widely endorsed by other schools as well as by leading riders in the competitive field. It is of course only a guide, the actual rate of progress varying considerably with the natural intelligence and ability of each individual horse. It can be described as follows:

Stage 1: First Year

Work on the Lunge   The objectives for this initial period of intimate contact (which lasts two or three months) with the young animal are to establish mutual confidence; to obtain mental, and subsequently physical, relaxation; to develop the muscular system and physical coordination; to familiarise the horse with training gear – the lunge-rein, the side-reins, the surcingle or saddle and the lunge whip; to establish a method of communication through the voice, the whip and the rein; to teach

Fig. 5 *Stage 1, first year – work on the lunge. Trainer remains on one spot; lunge rein taut, in line to elbow; side reins long enough to allow freedom of neck muscles.*

obedience to basic aids and words of command, and to establish an accepted system of rewards and punishments by the use of different tones of voice; to develop balance in the walk, trot and canter on the circle, without a rider; to teach the habit of learning and of attention; to establish confidence in the presence of the bit without risk of any pain or damage to the mouth; and, towards the end, the first introduction to the weight of the rider on the back. This constitutes a very busy and quite invaluable three months' programme that will prepare the horse for everything that is to follow.

Straight Forward Riding This means working the horse in as natural a position as possible, with a long rein and light contact, on straight lines and on gentle curves. The main objectives will be to cultivate mental calmness; to accustom the horse to carrying the weight of the rider on relaxed back-muscles; to give the horse time to further

Fig. 6 · *Stage 1, first year – straight forward riding. Simple work, without collection; mainly on straight lines; mostly rising when in trot; horse long and free.*

develop his muscles, especially in his back and neck, before being asked to do any intensive work under a rider and to establish the stability of the neck on the withers; to develop the horse's balance (now under a rider) in walk, trot and canter on straight lines and simple curves; to instil the habit of physical and mental cooperation and responsiveness to the basic aids of legs, reins, seat and voice.

Stage 2: Second to Third Year

The Lower School Sometimes called the Campagn School, this constitutes a sufficient education of the horse

*Fig. 7   Stage 2, second and third year – Lower (or Campagn) School.
Put to the aids; impulsion; towards collection; improved athletic rhythm;
all work more gymnastic; improved self-carriage.*

for all equestrian civilian or military purposes other than
the High School. The horse is put to the aids and taught
to move in self-carriage with impulsion and rhythm in all
normal school movements. Within those guidelines, the
horse is collected and also, still in self-carriage, taught to
lengthen and extend.

The process comprises mainly the stretching and
loosening of all muscles and their subsequent flexing and
suppling in collection. The hindquarters are engaged and
lowered to carry more weight and to facilitate the
collection. Freedom of limb and gymnastic agility is
established through work in all figures, turns and lateral
movements. The aim: a collected, supple and impulsive

horse, obedient and light on his feet and in the rider's hand.

Stage 3: Third and Fourth Year

The High School   This final phase involves the perfection and development to the ultimate degree of all the collected movements (the foundations of which have been laid in the earlier two stages) including piaffe, passage, pirouettes and one-time flying changes. All the basic rhythms should now contain the beautifying quality of cadence; suppleness should be absolute; and sub-

Fig. 8   *Stage 3, third and fourth year – the High School. Impulsion; submission; collection; confidence.*

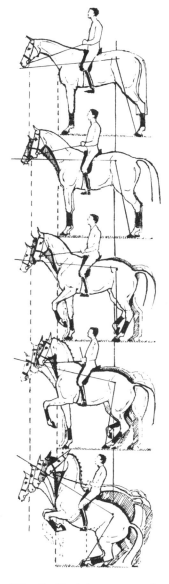

First year – straight forward riding.

Second year – Lower School balance.

Second/third year – Lower School collection; forwardness.

Third/fourth year – High School lightness; cadence.

Fourth year – ultimate balance and collection; forwardness.

Fig. 9   Training stages – the overall processes of improving balance and collection.

mission generously complete. The horse is completely trained for all airs on the ground and ready, if he shows the talent, for education in the airs above the ground, the levade, the capriole and the courbette. He is the complete and confident equine gymnast.

Essential Qualities
Calmness
This apparently simple quality is the foundation on which all dressage training is based, and without which it can hardly make any true progress. The horse, like the child, cannot learn unless he is attentive; but neither child nor horse will be attentive unless he is calm and relaxed in the mind, free from fear or anxiety. The achievement of calmness consequently becomes the dressage trainer's first task when he starts on the education of any young horse. It must take, and continue to take, priority over everything else.

Lack of calmness may exist from a number of causes: from temperamental instability; congenital nervousness; fear of human beings resulting from earlier maltreatment; too much rich and stimulating food; too little exercise; inexperience; or simple joie de vivre. Whatever the cause, the trainer has always to analyse it and then apply the appropriate treatment or antidote until such time as he can establish, or re-establish, a mutual confidence and its complementary calmness. Only then can he seriously expect to recommence instruction.

Lack of calmness implies mental tension, which in turn will always entail a degree of muscular or physical tension. But muscular tension is the antithesis of that muscular relaxation, or decontraction, that is the one vital prerequisite for the development of free movement. Since the whole purpose of dressage is to develop to the greatest possible extent the power and agility of a horse – both of which are unthinkable without maximum freedom of muscle and limb – so, as with ballet or human gymnastics, the preliminary loosening and stretching of muscles becomes essential. And for that there must be calmness.

Calmness is closely allied to obedience, and lack of calmness brings a corresponding lack of obedience. Any horse that is disobedient is anathema to any rider, and to none more than a dressage rider who requires a more refined type of obedience than others. The skills that are developed in a horse during dressage training are not tricks that he may do, or not do, just as he pleases. Everything he does, every muscle that he moves, is done at the specific behest and request of his rider – and should be done willingly and generously. Indeed, it has been said by the masters that nothing that a horse does entirely of his own accord is of any value, the validity of which sage remark being based on the appreciation of the fact that the horse does not possess the kind of intelligence that would lead him to work on his own to the maximum of his ability and power. He has therefore to learn to submit himself confidently, attentively and generously to the control of his rider, without resistance or any sense of resentment. All dressage training is difficult, but without that submission, which is founded on calmness, it becomes virtually impossible.

The chief corollary of submissive obedience is the constant willingness or desire of the horse to go forwards at the slightest sign from the rider, and with whatever degree of power or speed the rider calls for or permits. And when that is happening, we begin to see the perfect riding horse.

Forwardness
A horse that will not go forward with willingness and even generosity is of little value. The quality of forward-ness embodies the very essence of a horse, and without it

he can never be a pleasure to ride. It becomes the alpha and omega of all training.

Forwardness in a horse involves two factors:

(a) The horse must respond instantly to the lightest request by the rider to increase speed or length of stride, without hesitation or resentment. There must be no second thoughts or attitude of 'Will I, won't I?' But forwardness does not necessarily involve an increase in speed or length of stride: It is a quality that should and can be present in the horse's mind, even at the halt.

(b) The horse must have been taught to carry and use his body and limbs in such a manner that the whole of each and every impulsive action by his haunches both can and does flow forwards right through the muscles of his back, neck, shoulders and jaw, so that the rider feels his horse stepping forwards into his hands. That feeling will not occur if the forward flow of the action is stopped by the relative rigidity of back muscles that do not swing or by neck muscles that tend to hollow and become concave at the withers. The neck, like the back, should tend to lengthen and round itself with each impulsive thrust from the quarters.

The resulting forward flow of the impulsion, combined with the mental willingness to obey, produces a state of urgent mobility that we call 'forward'. Without it we have only half a horse.

Activity

Activity is of course the prerequisite of all forms of movement. It is represented by the energetic lifting of the horse's feet from the ground, albeit always in the required rhythm or sequence, whenever specific action is called for. It is the embryo of impulsion and can perhaps be likened to the light touch on the accelerator that a motorist gives just before he engages his clutch, to ensure that there is enough life in the engine to provide his getaway without stalling. In the same way the rider must activate his horse, or mobilise him in the sense that a peace-time army is mobilised for war. Good activity enables the rider to deploy his horse's energies in any way he wishes and, if required, to increase the tempo of a sluggish rhythm.

Suppleness

A horse, or any part of a horse, is supple when its muscles operate without any sign or sense of resistance or fixed contraction. When fully supple, the muscles should flex or contract so as to allow the horse the maximum freedom and use of his limbs and body when moving on a straight or curved line, and whether on one or on two tracks. A horse is said to be resisting when he consciously or even unconsciously stiffens one or more muscles in order to avoid complying fully with a request from his rider. In so doing, he makes himself – to a greater or lesser extent – disobedient. But since any form of disobedience is totally unacceptable in equitation, it is clear that complete suppleness in all parts of the horse is of prime and fundamental importance.

Submission

Submission, an essential quality in a good riding horse, should be interpreted as meaning that the horse is mentally willing and physically able to comply with his rider's requirements. He gives himself freely and generously to his rider. He does not try to intrude his own wishes above those of his rider. He cooperates in what becomes, in effect, a common or shared objective, and appears to enjoy doing so. Equestrian submission has nothing to do with a cowed obedience, although disobedience is the antithesis of submission. And without submission there can be no harmony. There is also a lack of submission when a horse stiffens one or more muscles in response to a request or an aid from the rider. Such a response implies resistance, and resistance is the negative of submission. It will be seen how closely related are the two qualities of suppleness and submission.

Straightness
Straightness in a horse is necessary for the purity and beauty of the paces and for the development of useable impulsion and collection. Impulsion deteriorates as soon as the horse makes himself crooked. Maximum impulsion is only possible in a straight horse. And without impulsion there can be no collection.

No horse is, by nature, absolutely straight in his body. All horses are found to have some degree of asymmetrical curvature in some part of their spine, even before they are backed or worked by human beings, and this asymmetry tends to set up unequal muscular development along the two sides. Left to himself, the horse will consequently tend to make himself concave and short on the one side and convex or long on the other. It is inevitable that the steps taken by the legs on the encurved side will be shorter and less free than those on the other, and vice versa. In the walk and the trot this means that the gait will be irregular and therefore impure. These discrepancies may be very slight and almost invisible, but they will affect the horse's performance.

The gait of the canter, fundamentally asymmetrical in any case, due to its three-beat sequence of footfall, tends further to encourage the natural encurvature of the horse when the canter-lead is on that side. When the lead is on the stiffer and naturally longer side, the horse will not be so apt to go crooked but there will be a certain awkwardness in the gait, due to the contradiction of the two asymmetries, ie the effect of the three-beat canter in one direction and the natural encurvature of the spine in the other. The rider can use these contradictory pulls in his efforts to overcome the natural crookedness of the horse's musculature.

It is the rider's constant endeavour, in his unending search for impulsion and purity, to make his horse straight. Conversely, the horse will constantly try, or tend, to move in a crooked manner because, that being natural as we have seen, it imposes less strain on his muscles, particularly those of his back. By allowing himself to remain crooked, he also avoids the extra muscle strain that would be imposed by the increased impulsion that the rider tries to engender. The self-interest of the horse and of the rider consequently lie in different directions.

The most visible expression of crookedness is that the horse's hindlegs are seen to follow a track that is not identical to the track of the forelegs. In order to overcome this false and debilitating position, it is essential that the rider should concentrate his efforts on placing and maintaining the forehand in the proper relationship to the hindquarters, that is to say in front of them. This is never easy to do, and it requires a considerable degree of prerequisite suppleness. However, little can be achieved by merely trying to push the quarters back into line behind the forehand, if only because such an exercise would entail the employment of the rider's legs solely to obtain a sideways movement of the erring quarters, at the expense of all forms of forward aiding. In that manner it would be impossible to hold the horse straight, even if some momentary improvement were obtained. In practice it will be found that the more the erring quarters are pushed out, the further out will the shoulders drift, with the result that the rider is always fighting a losing battle.

Straightening the horse by means of placing the forehand in front of the quarters necessitates the adoption

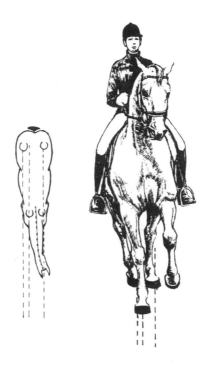

Fig. 10 (a) *Straightening – position left. Inner side of horse parallel to line of advance, with inside fore and hind feet on same track.*

of a progressive series of positions which enable, and indeed ensure, that the impulsive thrust of the hindlegs, and more particularly of the inside hindleg, passes forward straight through the horse's back to the forelimbs and into the neck and mouth. These progressive positions are known as Position left (or right); Shoulder-fore; and Shoulder-in. Together they form the main armoury for the rider's control of his horse's straightness and consequently of his power. Shoulder-in, first fully developed by Guerinière from some early studies by the Duke of Newcastle, in the eighteenth century, has become an established classic movement in its own right.

Fig. 10 (b) *Straightening –*
shoulder-fore. Horse's forehand
brought in line of inner hindleg;
horse moves on four tracks.

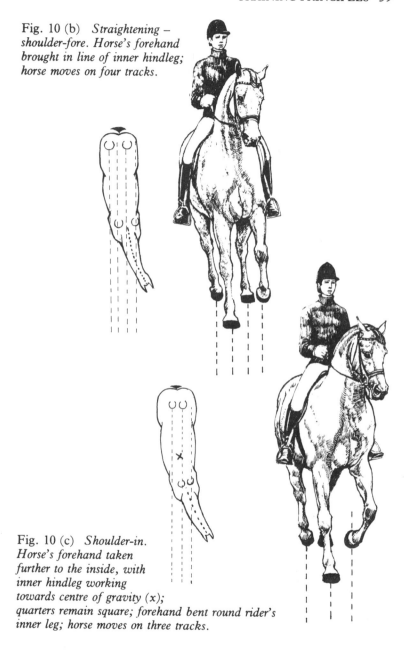

Fig. 10 (c) *Shoulder-in.*
Horse's forehand taken
further to the inside, with
inner hindleg working
towards centre of gravity (x);
quarters remain square; forehand bent round rider's
inner leg; horse moves on three tracks.

Self-carriage

As the result of training, the horse has to be taught to carry himself at all times in balance without relying on the reins and the rider's hands as a means of support for his forehand. This self-carriage can only be achieved gradually as the horse is trained to develop and exert the power of his quarters and especially of his loins to keep the forehand light. This is difficult and time-consuming, but it can be done, in·the same way as a man can strengthen and use his arm with sufficient power to lift a loaded shovel off the ground with only one hand.

The rider should at any time be able momentarily to release the contact with one or both reins without affecting the horse's balance and mobility, and without the horse reducing its impulsion or increasing its speed. The horse can then be said to be in self-carriage, being controlled by the rider's seat and legs and by the lightest touch of the reins.

Impulsion

Impulsion is energy, or power in action. It has little to do with speed though speed may result from it. Impulsion is inconceivable without a degree of containment, and can therefore be likened to the energy or power at the disposal of the yachtsman when he contains the wind in the sail of his boat; or of the child who contains the breeze in the body of his kite. If the wind is lost, the boat becomes unmanageable and the kite falls to the ground. But as long as the wind is contained, the boat and the kite can do wonderful things.

A racehorse galloping at speed on a loose rein has impetus, but no impulsion, because there is no containment of the energy; there is nothing to release. To be more specific and definitive, impulsion is energy from the quarters, passing through the horse's back, neck and poll, to be received into, contained, and directed by the hands of the rider, by means of the reins.

Impulsion is created mainly by the rider's legs, assisted to some extent by his seat. But it is a fact that neither the legs nor the seat have any mechanically compulsive power to create impulsion, or to cause the horse against his will to go forward with energy. The rein aids do have a mechanically compulsive power to produce certain results, if necessary against the horse's will; for example to cause him to deviate from a straight line or even to change his position from the halt. But seat and legs do not share that power, the horse having to be trained from the start to respond willingly, in certain preconceived ways, to what are at best merely conventional indications of what the rider requires him to do. No rider, by just increasing the pressure of his legs, can make an untrained horse move out of a halt, and even more surely not by any action that he may make with his back or seat-bones. The sudden infliction of pain is, of course, wholly excluded from this context.

As a result of careful and systematic training, the legs are able to demand and obtain impulsive activity from the horse's hindquarters. The seat, activated by the rider's loin muscles, is then able to modulate and to some extent direct the impulsive effect produced by the legs as it flows forward through the muscles of the horse's back, on which the seat is placed. But unless and until the back muscles are strong, supple and active, that is to say unless they are what is called swinging, the rider's seat is unable to play any significant part. The seat, in short, can have no effect whatever on a purely static back.

Balance
A horse is said to be balanced according to the extent to which he is able to maintain the distribution of his weight, together with that of his rider, in approximately equal proportions over his hindquarters and forehand.

With such a median distribution of his weight, he will be able to move with ease in any direction or at any speed or gait.

By nature and when standing still, about two thirds of a horse's total weight is carried by the forelegs and one third by the hindlegs. This uneven distribution is due to the fact that his conformation and normal posture provide nothing to counterbalance the weight of the head and neck that project at the front end and has to be carried entirely by the forehand. The inequality is further aggravated by the weight of the rider which is placed nearer to the withers than to the croup.

To make possible the neutralisation of the inconvenient effect of the rider, and thereafter to improve or equalise the distribution of the overall weight as between the forehand and the hindquarters, it is necessary to develop and strengthen the muscles of the horse's loin and back. These are the muscles that will ultimately enable the horse to lift his forehand off the ground as, for example, in a levade. But to begin with, the young horse will never have had any need to use them under stress and they will be undeveloped for anything more serious than playing around in a field. Their development takes time and the work must proceed slowly and patiently, the first stages taking place preferably during work on the lunge without a rider. Only when some progress has been made is it wise, or fair on the young horse, to impose the additional weight of the rider.

The progressive improvement of balance in a horse is achieved by gradually and systematically training him to engage his hindlegs and his hind-feet a little further forward than he will normally tend to do in an untrained state. For that engagement and adjusted posture, the muscles of the back and loin will have first to be stretched and flexed in the longitudinal plane, and the joints of the hindlegs taught to bend freely (Fig. 11).

Fig. 11 *Stretching exercise. The horse is ridden 'long and low' to stretch and free the muscles of his back and neck so that they can thereafter be strengthened and kept supple. The back can then swing and the quarters can be engaged. The horse remains on the bit with, in view of the angle of the neck, his head a little behind the vertical.*

Beyond a certain point, the acquisition of better balance turns into the acquisiton of collection, as and when the hindquarters begin to carry more weight than the forehand. This is merely one more example of the interplay and interrelationship of many fundamental qualities that we need to search for and develop in dressage training. In this particular case, the ultimate in balance and collection in motion is a correct piaffe in which the great majority of the weight is carried on the quarters, leaving the forehand very light and free. The ultimate in stationary balance and collection is the levade, in which the entire weight is carried on the haunches, the forehand being held motionless above the ground.

On the Bit

If a horse is to be fully controllable he must, in all his gaits and paces, in all his work, and even at the halt or when reining-back, be on the bit. This is without doubt the most essential, inescapable and permanently demanding principle in the gymnastic-training curriculum. It is written clearly and unequivocally into the Official Rules for Dressage, with the requirements elaborated in some detail. It is so important that it will be wise to start this discussion by quoting the relevant paragraph of the Rules in full.

Rules Definition   'In all his work, even at the halt, the horse must be "on the bit". A horse is said to be "on the bit" when the neck is more or less raised and arched according to the stage of training and the extension or collection of the pace, and he accepts the bridle with a soft contact and submissiveness throughout. The head should remain in a steady position, as a rule slightly in front of the vertical, with a supple poll at the highest point of the neck, and no resistance should be offered to the rider.'

Practical Application   That paragraph sets out in brief outline what the rider should feel and the spectator see, but it would be a mistake to think that that is all there is to it. The appearance of the horse as just described is merely the end result of the application of certain geometric, mechanical and biological laws which together enable the rider to develop, make use of, and control the full potential of his horse in terms of power and gymnastic ability. So long as the horse is not on the bit, his full power and ability will not be developed; it will consequently not be made use of; and what there is of it will most certainly not be easily controlled. Conversely, when the horse is in all respects on the bit, the rider discovers that almost anything is possible. Obviously it is desirable to understand how those geometric, mechanical and physical laws function, otherwise they will not be properly applied and the end result will be correspondingly marred. The Rules do not provide that information.

Up to the Bit It is necessary, before discussing those laws in detail, to interpolate one additional factor. It is not sufficient for the horse to present the correct outline or picture as described in the Rules. If that was all that occurred, the action would be somewhat passive and ineffective. We have to remember that the horse works from his quarters forwards, and for the action to be effective, positive and productive, it is essential that he should work up to the bit (or forward to the bit). If he is not up to the bit, he will be behind the bit, a situation that can be likened to driving a car with a badly slipping clutch. Assuming that the horse is working up to the bit, and that all the prescribed aspects of being on the bit are present, we find ourselves entering the sphere of impulsion which has already been discussed in Chapter 4. Impulsion is the fuel of gymnastic ability, but if the horse is not both on and up to the bit, there can be no containment, and so no impulsion. Therein lies the reason, the importance and the necessity for the horse, in all his work, to be 'on the bit'.

Geometry, Mechanics and Angles We have said that the methods employed in causing a horse to work on and up to the bit involve certain laws of geometry and mechanics, and we must now look at how they work. A glance at the drawings in Fig. 12 will make this easy. It is very largely

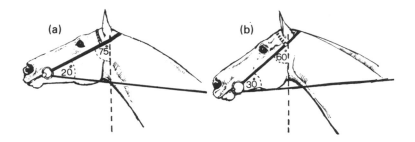

Fig. 12 *On the bit.*
(a) *Not on the bit; extremely bad; uncontrollable.*
(b) *Not on the bit; very bad.*
(c) *Not on the bit; bad.*
(d) *Not on the bit; fairly bad.*
(e) *Not on the bit; insufficient.*
(f) *Just on the bit; sufficient.*
(g) *On the bit; good.*
(h) *On the bit; good for maximum collection.*
(i) *Overbent.*

a matter of two angles, and these are shown on each of the drawings. They are the angle between the rein and the horse's jaw; and the angle of the horse's face to a vertical line drawn through the poll. The logic and the effect of these angles will be discussed in the following paragraphs, but it can be summarised by saying that, in general terms, the angle of the rein to the jaw should be as large as possible; and that the angle of the head to the vertical should be as small as possible. When such angles apply, leverage is greatest at both ends of the head, with resulting lightness of control by the rider, in addition to certain physical benefits that will accrue to the horse's performance.

It will be seen from the drawings that as the angle of the head to the vertical becomes larger than the ideal – Fig. 12 (g) and (h) – so the angle of the rein and jaw becomes smaller and there will inevitably be an increasing

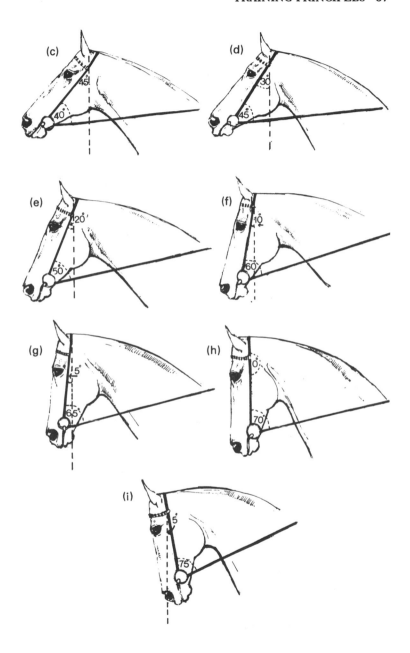

tendency for the tension on the bit to slide upwards, along the jaw, so that ultimately it begins to operate backwards through the neck muscles, ie by the same route along which the waves of impulsion should be travelling forward. The free, forward flow is therefore interrupted and is blocked at the withers; the elasticity of the neck muscles is lost; and the horse's back becomes more or less rigid. Gymnastic ability is destroyed. See Fig. 12 (f)–(a), in that order, and especially (a).

Leverage   If, on the other hand, the head line is maintained at only slightly in advance of the vertical – Fig. 12 (g) – the rein tension remains steadily on the lower areas of the jaw where it tends to bring the head even nearer to the vertical because of the leverage it can exert in that position, acting directly to the rider's hand. The muscular impulsion from the quarters can then continue to flow uninterruptedly through the back, neck, poll and jaw to the controlling reins, the head acting as a relatively soft and elastic lever between the bit and the poll. In this way, the vital elasticity of the back is retained and the horse is thereby enabled to function with maximum efficiency. He can now push himself up to the bit without stiffening or obstruction and will be able to accept collection without force or stress.

We have to remember that the horse has enormous power which he can use against his rider's wishes – if he is allowed to – with devastating effect. He is also very adept at finding means of doing just that, especially when he thinks that such action will enable him to work less hard. But the rider has a better understanding of mechanics than the horse and he will be greatly assisted by the employment, albeit always with tact, of the additional power provided by the several leverages we have mentioned.

For the horse to move efficiently it is necessary for him

to be free of stiffness in all his muscles and joints, and most particularly in the muscles of the back, neck, and the joint of the poll, all of which are closely related. The position of the horse's head, and the resulting angle of the poll, has a major influence on the back and neck muscles. Broadly speaking, the smaller the angle of the poll, or the nearer the head is to the vertical, the freer will be the neck and back muscles, provided only that the swing of the muscles is not forcibly restricted by excessive or harsh use of the reins.

The worst thing that can occur is when the horse manages, or is allowed, to stick his nose more or less straight out in front, with the face approaching the horizontal – Fig. 12 (a). In that position, the poll and neck become virtually rigid, no lever works, and the rider is helpless.

Rider Control The lower angle, that between the rein and the jaw, is of at least equal importance. As the drawings will show, the greater the angle, the greater will be the influence and the control that the rider will have over the position of the head itself and over the subsequent action and play of the all important and interrelated muscles of neck, back, quarters and hindlegs. From this interrelated play the rider can ultimately develop the very sophisticated relationship between the influence of the reins and the activity of the hindlegs, a relationship referred to often by Colonel Podhajski as the 'cycle of the rein aids going through the horse'.

Cycle of the Aids This cycle of the rein aids can be explained in another way:

(a) Muscular activity and impulsion start in the hindlegs and quarters, proceeding through the loins, back and neck to the poll.

(b) With the head held near the vertical at the poll, the impulsion meets no obstruction in that area from the tension of the reins and carries the horse forward in freedom of movement.

(c) With the poll supple and unresistant, the forward thrust is felt and controlled in an elastic manner by the rein contact on the bars of the mouth, the wide rein angle there helping to keep the bit steady on the bars.

(d) The leverage of the two angles on the poll joint keep it supple and elastic.

(e) The impulsion is thus taken up by the rider's hands, passes through his forearms to the elbows and thence, by way of the light contact between elbow and upper part of the pelvis, to the seat-bones, the back muscles of the horse and the quarters.

(f) The cycle is thus completed, with no inhibition to the impulsive flow.

Conversely, the rein cycle is impossible if the horse is not on the bit, because the impulsion would then never reach the mouth and would therefore never reach the rider's hands. Look again at the extreme case shown in Fig. 12 (a). We have already noted that that particular set of angles, wide at the poll and narrow at the mouth, results in a stiffening of all the muscles of the neck and back. The narrow angle at the mouth results in the main rein tension coming back along the neck to the withers where it meets the forward-flowing impulsion. A blockage results to the detriment of all suppleness. The quarters and hindlegs are in no way influenced by the rein effects. This tendency of the rein tension to flow back through the neck is acute and disastrous in Fig. 12 (a). It gets progressively less as the head gets nearer to the vertical (comes onto the bit) and is non-existent in the ideal position of Fig. 12 (g) or (h).

The section under the heading Durchlässigkeit (page 75) is very relevant to the cycle of the aids.

Overbent   Any tendency of the horse's head to come behind the vertical – Fig. 12 (i) – must be regarded in normal circumstances as a danger signal and is most undesirable. The horse is then regarded as being overbent, to the detriment of his work and freedom of action. Increasingly, as the extent of the angle behind the vertical increases, the horse's throat, gullet and windpipe are restricted and the neck is forced into a false and excessive bend. It will no longer be possible for the rider to push the horse up to the bit as he will tend to avoid the demand by going over the top of it and, ultimately, leaning on it.

There is, however, one set of circumstances which are exceptional to the rule that behind the vertical is overbent. The exercise of stretching the horse's spine, right through the back and the neck, forwards and downwards to the extent that the nose comes at least as low as the level of the chest and even down to the knees, is extremely valuable at all stages of training. Its purpose is to elongate and free from any form of restraint or contraction all the muscles along the top-line of the horse so that they can then be made supple and their elasticity maintained. It counteracts the almost inevitable tendency of the horse's back to flatten and stiffen under the stress of constantly being asked to do difficult things under the weight of the rider.

When this stretching exercise is done correctly the angle of the head to the neck should be allowed to remain more or less as it was when the horse was carrying himself normally with his neck between 20 and 40 degrees above the horizontal. It follows that when the neck is taken down to well below the horizontal, the horse *still remaining on and up to the bit*, the face-line will come behind the vertical. In that position, he is not overbent because there will be nothing forced or restrictive about the angle at the poll, which, together with the flexion of the first two neck vertebrae, remains more or less as it was before. On the other hand, if the horse, when his head is low, should be allowed to poke his nose forward, on to or in front of the vertical, the effect on the back muscles will be similar to that of the nose-poking that we have seen in Fig. 12 (a); that is to say, the muscles of the back will begin to flatten and the chief object of the exercise will be lost.

The important points to remember when employing this exercise are:

(a) The horse must remain on the bit so that he can be ridden, or pushed, down by the rider and not just allowed to go down if, when and as he wishes.

(b) The neck must be encouraged to stretch forward as well as down, and never pulled in or back. There must be no forced bend in the neck itself.

(c) Gentle impulsion must be maintained by the rider's legs to encourage engagement of the hindlegs.

This stretching exercise can be used with great advantage at any time in the course of a daily work-out; certainly at the beginning before serious work commences; often in the middle to relieve physical and nervous tensions; and very beneficially at the end to ensure that the horse returns to the stable at peace in body and mind.

Conclusion The state of being on the bit may perhaps be summed up by saying that it represents a set of conditions by which the horse is most fully and easily controlled but is also, at the same time, most able to place himself, together with his full power and potential, at his rider's disposal. He gives himself, and all that is his, to his rider.

If the horse is not on the bit (Fig. 12 (f), (g) and (h)), he is either above the bit (Fig. 12 (a), (b), (c), (d) and (e)), or over the bit – overbent (Fig. 12 (i)). In addition if he is not up to the bit, he will be behind the bit.

Losgelassenheit and Durchlässigkeit

We have to acknowledge that the English language is not always the most efficient medium for expressing or explaining some of the more subtle aspects of the dressage ethos. It may in some ways be superior in its flexibility to the German or the French, especially perhaps where such closely related matters as rhythm, cadence and tempo are concerned. But in other respects it can become distinctly inferior and virtually tongue-tied when compared with the German. The latter can benefit immeasurably from its well-known ability to mould several words into one and, in doing so, to endow the resulting composite word with an immediately recognisable meaning that is greater than the sum of its parts.

It not infrequently happens that it is simply not possible to provide a direct and intelligible English translation to such composite German words. Inevitably we then come up against a major problem when the German composite refers to some vital and indispensable aspect of dressage training. We cannot afford, as already pointed out in the preface to this book, to by-pass or ignore the subject even though we are unable to provide a suitable word or phrase in our own language that will be generally and appropriately understood to mean the same thing. Usually, British horsemen try to bridge the communication-gap by the use of some quite inadequate word that fails in its purpose because it hardly means anything in particular. Inevitably, then, the word itself, and indeed the whole subject in question, suffers increasing neglect, to the ultimate and great disadvantage of British dressage.

The disadvantage that the British suffer in this matter of intercommunication about a subject on which almost all the important and original research has been done in foreign countries is exacerbated by the fact that we, as individuals and as a nation, have subsequently failed to carry out any detailed research of our own. Our knowledge, both theoretical and practical, is relatively superficial. With several hundred years of neglect behind us, we are in no position to try and ignore the problem and go it alone. We desperately need to learn from the Germans and the French and to do that we must at least learn to understand the logic and the real meaning and implication of the German words. The French present fewer problems because they do not use composites.

There are two German words which stand at the head of the list of near-incomprehensibles, and both are of outstanding importance in dressage. They are Losgelassenheit and Durchlässigkeit. They are not directly related, though each has some bearing on the other. We can therefore study them separately.

Losgelassenheit This composite word has three integral elements: (a) LOS – this has to do with freedom in the sense of something being loose or unrestricted and on-going, as a dog released from its chain. Curiously, this word is fairly common currency with British shooting men who often encourage their gun-dogs to search for game with cries of 'hey-los' or just 'los'. (b) GELASSEN – this is simply the past-participle of the verb *lassen* – to allow. (c) HEIT – is a suffix which implies that the previous elements have been bound together and operate in such a way that they are recognisable as a specific quality or manner. The nearest direct equivalent in English would be the word-ending 'ness', for example in softness or happiness.

Putting those three elements together, we begin to see that we are talking about a quality of free, on-going and uninhibited action. With that in mind, we remember that the first lesson that has to be established in the work of any dressage horse is the requirement that the animal should learn to move with all his muscles and limbs operating in a free, forward-going and unconstrained manner. It is a combination of those qualities that we wish to feel and to see permeating every part of the horse. There must be no stiffening and no withholding. It is that combination of qualities that is so well covered by the single German word *Losgelassenheit*. Everything is being allowed its full freedom. The word fills the bill admirably and can be introduced into any sentence without causing a disturbance. But an effort to translate that word into an even moderately concise English phrase will produce cumbersome results, likely to lead to vagueness or, more probably, to confusion. We need the German word and we should therefore digest its meaning, accept it, and get used to using it as we have done for many centuries with so many French words.

Durchlässigkeit The key to this second three-element word lies in the first syllable, *Durch* – through. *Durchlassen* would be translated as 'to let, or allow through'. But our word is not spelt like that, the Germans having used a variation of *lassen* (*lässig*) to form a permanent word in its own right (*durchlässig*), which is directly translatable as 'permeable'. Again, as in *losgelassenheit*, the suffix implies a quality and turns the adjective into an abstract noun.

In English, if something is permeable it is also pervious, implying that it can be permeated by or passed through by other matter. A cotton coat is not impervious, or impermeable, to rain. *Durchlässigkeit*, turned into rather basic English, therefore can be called the quality of permeability. But the one word 'permeability' alone would hardly suffice to form the basis of a very important equestrian truth.

One of the highest aims of fine horsemanship is to achieve a state of training; a state of mutual harmony and communication between horse and rider; in which the slightest aid or message issuing from any part of the rider's body whether it be his hands, his legs, his seat or his weight, shall pass into and through, and shall affect, the whole of the horse. There must be no barrier or blockage causing the message to receive response only from certain limited areas. The response should be clearly felt to be coming from the entire physical and mental being of the horse. The horse listens and then responds with the whole of himself. To use the fewest possible words, we have a situation when *the aids go through the horse*, from one end to the other. They permeate the permeable horse. We have *Durchlässigkeit*.

Under such blissful circumstances, the hind-feet will be affected and drawn forward by the restraining rein aid; an urging-forward aid from the rider's seat will cause the horse to press up to the rider's hands with a rounded, soft back and flexed poll. The permeability will work in both directions and at the same time.

As with *Losgelassenheit*, our equestrian language will benefit very greatly if we can accept the word *Durchlässigkeit* into common usage as a valuable and intelligible word in its own right.

5: The Paces and Gaits – How the Horse Progresses

The human species, being biped, has only one basic form of progression, comprising the placing in turn of each of his two legs (hindlegs) in front of the other. If, as part of each forward step, he incorporates a little jump during which, for an instant, neither foot is on the ground, we say that he is running instead of walking, but the principle of transferring weight from one foot to the other remains the same.

The horse, and many other quadrupeds, have several quite distinct methods of procedure that we call gaits and which he can adopt according to his requirements from time to time. All are perfectly natural and it is therefore necessary, according to universal dressage philosophy, to develop and improve each and all of them so as to produce a complete horse and to preserve the full nature of the animal.

The natural gaits of the horse are the Walk, the Trot, the Canter and the Gallop. The first three are entirely different from each other, but there is a recognisable relationship between the last two, the canter and the gallop, the latter being a logical development of the former brought about by additional speed. In the French language, the dressage usage of the word *Galop* refers to the canter and not to the real gallop. The true gallop gait is never included in any dressage competition or display, if only because of the limitations of the normally available space. Dressage training is therefore concerned with the development and display of a horse in the three basic gaits of Walk, Trot and Canter, each in their various forms or airs.

It has become conventional, in order to demonstrate their full gymnastic potential, to work horses in several variations or degrees of each of the basic gaits. These are:

In walk: collected walk, medium walk and extended walk.
In trot: collected trot, working trot, medium trot and extended trot.
In canter: collected canter, working canter, medium canter and extended canter.

These variations refer, in the main, to the degree of length of the stride and, to some extent, also to the length of the overall frame in which the horse executes the work. The particular variation of gait used at any given time will be dictated by the standard or level of training at which the work is being done.

It will be seen that one alone of the three gaits, the walk, is not practised in the working variety. This is because of the extreme difficulty encountered in endeavouring to modulate this intricate gait sufficiently to show four distinct variations without adversely affecting the purity of the gait in at least one of them. In any case, the working variation is seldom employed in any of the gaits at the more advanced levels of training.

Each working gait should be interpreted as being one of moderate degree in which the horse can work for prolonged periods without strain. Each medium gait should be interpreted as one of mild extension.

All dressage consists of a series of variations, in the musical sense of that word, on the three themes of walk, trot and canter. The higher the level of test or display, the more subtle and intricate will be the interplay of those variations, though always the absolute purity of the three basic gaits, the absolute regularity and correctitude of their footfall sequence, should be given priority over all other considerations. There should also be a consistent and easily recognisable relationship between the tempi in which the gaits are executed, and each variation should be immediately and clearly recognisable for what it is.

The Walk

In a correct walk, each of the four feet come to the ground separately and with absolute regularity and consistency of sequence. The sequence of one complete stride of four steps would consist, for example, of the near-hind followed by the near-fore, the off-hind and the off-fore in that order.

In the collected walk, the steps should be comparatively short and elevated with the result that the ground-fall of the hind-feet will be some way short of the imprints of the fore-feet. The steps become progressively longer and

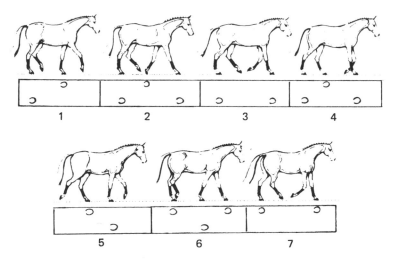

Fig. 13 (a) *The walk (true). A true walk has regularly recurring moments (see Figs 3 and 7) when both legs on one side slope towards each other; a four-beat gait with no moment of suspension.*

Fig. 13 (b)   *Collected walk. Shortened steps; increased elevation; no track-up of hindlegs.*

less elevated with the medium and the extended walks until, covering as much ground as possible in the latter, the ground-fall of the hind-feet will be well in front of or beyond the imprints of the fore-feet.

In collection, the neck is raised and arched. In extension it is lowered and lengthened, the horse remaining lightly on the bit with continuous rein contact. In all variations of the walk gait, movement of the limbs should be active, clear and 'marching'.

Any breakdown in the regularity of the correct sequence of footfall will cause the walk to become increasingly like an amble, characterised by both legs on the same side appearing to swing forward at more or less the same time, as it were in parallel and as is clearly seen with camels and often with dogs. An amble is not a walk and is consequently regarded as a grave fault.

In a true walk a spectator should be able to recognise a

Fig. 13 (c) *Medium walk. Marching forward; moderate elevation; full track-up or some over-track.*

Fig. 13 (d) *Extended walk. Maximum length of stride; good over-track; least elevation; energetic; free swing of the shoulder; horse maintains steady contact with the rein.*

Fig. 14 *The amble. A false walk in which the two legs on one side appear to move more or less in parallel to each other. In full amble the horse will be moving in two-time instead of four-time.*

tendency for the two legs on the same side to swing in opposite directions to each other. This tendency can be seen in Fig. 13 (a), parts 1, 2, 3, 5, 6 and 7.

The walk is a difficult gait to master in all its aspects, not least because its regularity and perfection can very easily be upset by incompetent or insensitive riding and by mental tension in the horse. Very few competitors, even at World Championship level, are able to show a good walk in all three variations, a well performed collected walk being the most rarely seen. In the latter case, the gait all too frequently is either insufficiently collected, or the tempo becomes too slow and lethargic, or the tendency to amble becomes apparent.

The Trot
In a good trot, each diagonal pair of legs make a simultaneous ground-fall, thus making a regular and

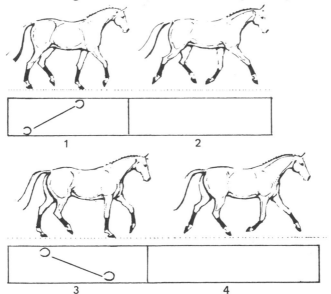

Fig. 15 (a) *The trot. A two-beat gait regularly repeated and on alternate diagonals, with a brief moment of suspension between beats.*

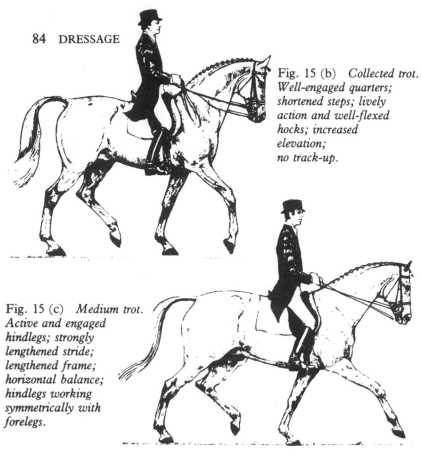

Fig. 15 (b)   *Collected trot.*
Well-engaged quarters;
shortened steps; lively
action and well-flexed
hocks; increased
elevation;
no track-up.

Fig. 15 (c)   *Medium trot.*
Active and engaged
hindlegs; strongly
lengthened stride;
lengthened frame;
horizontal balance;
hindlegs working
symmetrically with
forelegs.

Fig. 15 (d)   *Extended trot.*
Maximum length of stride; well-
engaged hocks and hindlegs working
symmetrically with forelegs; free
action of shoulder; lengthened frame,
including neck; toe of foreleg points
towards point of impact; balance
horizontal; rider remains
upright and
balanced
with still
legs.

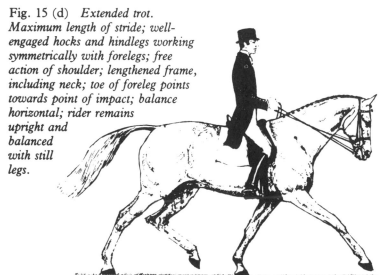

Fig. 15 (e) *Extended trot (in suspension). Big over-track after prolonged suspension resulting from maximum thrust from hindleg and length of stride.*

equal two-time beat to each full stride. It is of the essence of the trot that there should be sufficient swing through the body at each step to produce a discernible moment of total suspension between the footfalls of the two diagonal pairs of legs (Fig. 15 (a) 2 and 4). If this moment of suspension did not exist it would be impossible for the horse to lengthen his stride beyond a certain point without interfering with the sequence or damaging himself by striking one hind-foot against the fore-foot on the same side. The easy and simple symmetry of the trot makes it the most fundamental of the three gaits for the overall training and development of the horse and for the production of balance, suppleness and impulsion.

As with the walk, the steps are comparatively short and elevated in collection, lengthening appreciably in

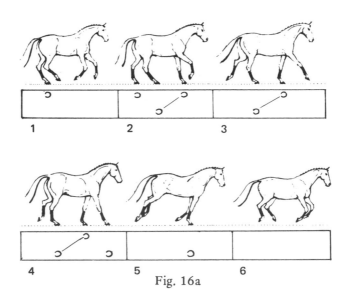

Fig. 16a

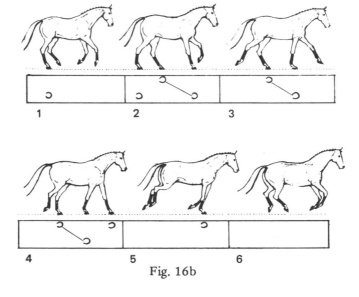

Fig. 16b

medium, and covering the maximum amount of ground in extension. The working variation is a steady, moderate and active form for prolonged work that demands neither collection nor the beginnings of extension. The marks of the hind-feet will fall behind those of the fore-feet in collection, but will be in advance of them in medium and markedly so in extension in which form there will consequently be a prolonged period of total suspension.

In collection, the quarters are very slightly lowered as the result of increasingly flexed and engaged hindlegs, while in extension the horse becomes horizontal and somewhat longer and less arched in the neck. It is of particular importance that in extension the front- and hindlegs should act, and be seen to act, in complete harmony and with an equally shared amount of freedom and activity. To achieve this harmony, the well-flexed hindlegs must come well forward under the horse so that the lower part, between the hock and the fetlock, appears to be parallel to the fully extended foreleg of the same diagonal when fully extended.

The Canter
The canter, with its asymmetrical three-beat strides, and with the additional impulsion produced by the coordinated use of both hindlegs, is perhaps the most exciting of the three basic gaits. It has an easily visible moment of total suspension between each successive stride.

A correct canter stride is initiated by one hindleg, followed by the other hindleg acting in simultaneous conjunction with its diagonal foreleg, and ending with the ground-fall of the remaining or leading foreleg. As in

Fig. 16 Opposite: *The canter. A three-beat gait with clear moment of full suspension. The fore- and hindlegs on the same side will always appear to be leading their opposites. (a) Canter right (off-side legs leading). (b) Canter left (near-side legs leading).*

Fig. 16 (c)   *Collected canter. Engaged quarters; weight evenly distributed; perfect balance.*

Fig. 16 (d)   *Highly collected canter (eg before a pirouette). Very well-
engaged quarters with highly flexed hocks; forehand very light.*

Fig. 16 (e) *Medium canter. Lengthened frame and stride; good horizontal balance.*

Fig. 16 (f) *Extended canter. Free, lengthened stride with lengthened frame; balance maintained.*

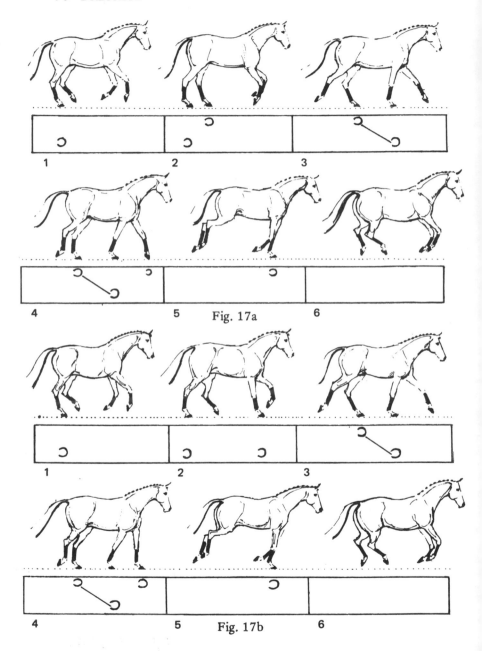

Fig. 17a

Fig. 17b

the walk, there is a constant changing of the number of feet that are carrying weight on the ground at any given moment during the course of the stride, the mechanics of which amount to a roll-over process that commences with just the one initiating hindleg, passes over the other three and ultimately ends with only the leading foreleg on the ground, carrying the entire weight on its own as did the initiating hindleg at the beginning. Then follows the moment of full suspension before the process repeats. A good canter is characterised by a fine impulsion resulting in a clear, bold rhythm and a hardly audible lightness of footfall. Any deficiency of engagement is likely to result in a heavy, hesitant or slightly rolling action or, in extreme cases, in the appearance of a four-time beat in the footfall due to the front and rear feet of the second (diagonal) phase ceasing to be simultaneous; in effect, either the hindleg or the foreleg of the diagonal comes to the ground, in a hurried manner, before its counterpart. Both varieties of failure destroy the validity of the canter – see Fig. 17 (a) part 2 and Fig. 17 (b) part 2.

The main problem inherent in the canter, as already noted in the section on impulsion, is the difficulty of keeping the hindlegs in precisely the same track as the forelegs, due to the natural asymmetry of the gait and the consequent tendency of the horse to have a less than symmetrical dorsal development. There is always, even with the straightest horses, a tendency for them to swing the quarters in towards the side of the leading leg, thus diminishing the possibility of full impulsion flowing right through the horse.

To maintain impulsion and lightness in the canter, it is essential that the hindleg that initiates the stride should

Fig. 17 Opposite: *Incorrect canter (four-time). (a) Hurried hindleg; (b) Hurried foreleg.*

engage well forward under the horse in the direction of the centre of gravity. The rest will then follow with comparative ease because the horse will then be better balanced with a more even distribution of weight as between the forehand and the quarters.

All competition tests invariably specify the leg, either right or left, on which the horse is required to lead in canter, and also the points in the arena at which he is required to change the lead. It is conventional to refer normally to the leading foreleg of a canter although in fact, as may be seen in the illustrations, it would be equally valid to refer to the leading hindleg. For example, when a horse is leading with the right foreleg he

Fig. 18 *The halt. Square; collected; forward; attentive; immobile.*

is bound also, if the canter is correct, to be leading with the right hindleg, ie the right fore- and hindlegs will strike the ground after and in front of their opposites, both having previously been simultaneously in suspension.

The Halt
The halt should demonstrate perfect immobility, which implies perfect balance, and also perfect readiness for instant mobility in any required direction. For the former, the horse must stand absolutely square on his four feet with his weight evenly distributed. He must remain lightly but firmly on the bit, with impulsion implied by his mental state of attention. For the latter, the state of readiness for action, the hindlegs must be well collected and engaged, the forehand relatively light, thus providing him with the ability to respond instantly to any request to move with a clear step by his hindlegs which should always initiate every forward movement. There should be no need for any shuffling intermediary step before he can execute the first full step of walk, trot, canter or rein-back.

The horse should always move into the halt with precision, smoothly, promptly and in perfect balance. To achieve this the horse must be caused to close himself up into the halt, from the back towards the front, and must never give the appearance of having been pulled back into the halt by the reins. The movement should not appear rough or abrupt, although there should be no unnecessary or uncalled-for steps.

The Rein-back
All horses are severely limited in their ability to move backwards by the design given them by nature for their skeletal and muscular framework. Biologically, the shape, size and position of every joint and group of

(a)

Fig. 19 *The rein-back. A two-beat, or almost two-beat, movement by diagonals. The foreleg has always to initiate the movement for the first stride back.*

muscles has evolved into a pattern that contributes towards the horse's ability to move forwards with ease, efficiency and speed, to escape from his natural enemies. But when he tries to move backwards, the joints and muscles cannot operate with the same or comparable efficiency, the action becoming somewhat awkward. He can only move backwards slowly and with considerable difficulty. Instead of propelling himself forwards, he has to pull or draw himself backwards. We have also to bear in mind that, when reining-back, the horse cannot see where he is going or where he is putting his feet, and this must inevitably test his confidence in himself and in his rider.

Left to himself, the horse will not use the backward

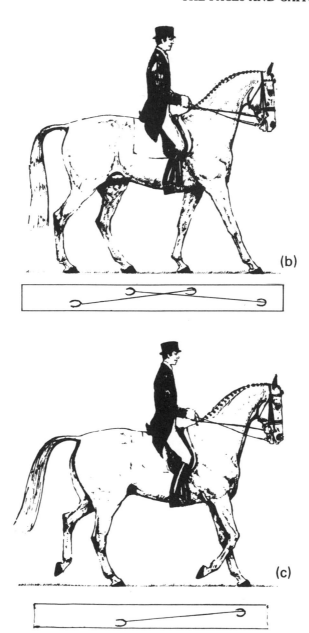

(b)

(c)

method of movement very often, and never for more than a few strides although he can, if not hurried or forced, continue backwards for considerably longer distances than that without harm or undue strain. It is interesting to note that, to help maintain his balance in this awkward and 'blind' movement, the horse adopts a gait in which he alternates between two and four feet on the ground at all times – Fig.19 (a)–(c).

The awkwardness is demonstrated by the fact that the horse is forced to adopt an entirely different gait from that which he uses for any forward movement. He cannot manage any form of jump between steps and so, there being no period of suspension, the action cannot be said to resemble either a trot or a canter. Neither can he conveniently organise his legs in a regular four-time sequence as in the forward walk. In fact, he can only move backwards with comfort by adopting a more or less accurately synchronised two-time sequence in which the opposite diagonals, the off-fore/near-hind and the near-fore/off-hind, move together in a regular and noticeably unhurried rhythm although, at best, it tends to lack grace.

The basic problem is that the forehand, which is at the rear of the movement, has little propelling power in any direction while the hindquarters – and especially the hocks, due to the direction in which the joints flex – lose almost all their immense power in the backward direction. Nevertheless, when used with discretion and without force, the rein-back constitutes a fine exercise for the horse's loins and consequently for his ability to collect himself. It is also good mental training, helping to ensure and maintain mental submission and to control any tendency to excessive ardour.

Finally, the rein-back should always be achieved as the result of forward impulsion from the quarters that has been restrained in the rider's hands. It should never be the result of a backward pull on the reins, though this requirement is often neglected.

Transitions

All transitions from one gait or variation of a gait to another must, like the transition into the halt already described, be made promptly, clearly and precisely when called for, but they must also be smooth and not abrupt. Throughout the transition, whether upwards to a higher speed or downwards to a lower one, the horse should remain light in hand, calm and consistently on the bit. The same requirements apply when making a transition from one movement or air to another, eg from the passage into an extended trot or into a piaffe.

6: Dressage Movements –
Their Good and Bad Points

General

All dressage movements are ridden for one or more of several quite clear and positive purposes. They may form an exercise designed simply to strengthen or to supple the horse, the former more especially in his back and hindquarters and the latter especially in his neck, poll, mouth and shoulders. They may be used to increase the horse's intelligence, obedience and gymnastic dexterity. And finally they can be used, in competition or in displays, to make attractive patterns on the ground and to show off the skill of the rider, the developed beauty of the horse, and the harmonious relationship between the two parties. The last purpose is probably the ultimate aim of all dressage in the twentieth century because a high-class display by a polished horseman on a well-trained horse invariably gives immense pleasure to even quite uninitiated spectators. It also gains the rider a good deal of prestige and, occasionally, substantial prizes.

Many movements within the dressage curriculum can be, and usually are, ridden in all three of the basic gaits of walk, trot and canter. Others are inherently concerned with only one gait as, for example, the flying change of leg (canter), the piaffe (a trot form) and the passage (trot form). The opportunities for the inventive creation of floor patterns, with the interplay of the main available movements and gaits, are almost unlimited, as they are in ballroom-dancing or skating. The effect of such patterns can in addition be enhanced by the introduction of appropriate musical accompaniment.

Straight Lines

The importance of straightness in a horse cannot be overestimated, not least because of the undoubtedly strong aesthetic factor involved. In purely practical terms, any lack of straightness immediately results in a weakening of impulsion and consequently of overall efficiency; of the regularity and purity of the gait; and of the rider's ability to remain in full control of his horse. If the straightness is flawed, the performance as a whole is flawed in its aesthetic impression as well as in its technical details.

Straightness lies in the controlled and directly related positioning of the horse's hindquarters and forehand, through the back. A horse is said to be straight when he is equally supple on both sides and when his hindlegs are following on the same line as his forelegs. Only then can the horse be balanced and relaxed. Only then can true collection be achieved. And only then can his back swing naturally for the greater use and deeper pleasure of his rider.

The straightness of a horse can best be appreciated during the course of any movement executed along, or closely parallel to, the centre line of an arena, and especially by a judge or spectator who is located near to one end of the centre line. Any deviation of the horse's quarters from the line followed by the forehand, or any false curvature of the spine or neck, will then be most clearly observed.

The ability or failure of the rider to overcome the quite natural tendency of his horse to be less than straight is, on the other hand, best appreciated when the horse is moving along the track on the long side of an arena. Under those circumstances the width of the horse's quarters being greater than that of the forehand, there will be an additional tendency to crookedness as the horse tries to keep the outer side of his body parallel to the wall or boards. He will try to place his fore-feet exactly the same distance from the wall as his hind-feet. It consequently becomes the rider's job to take appropriate measures to counteract the instinctive if slight crookedness of his horse, due entirely to the natural wedge-shape of his conformation, by causing him to move with his fore-feet slightly further away from the wall than the hind-feet; in fact, by bringing the forehand in a little. And this is not easy.

In classical dressage, with this point in mind, the horse should always be ridden in such a position that the inner side of his body, the side furthest away from the wall, appears to be parallel to the wall. This is called riding in position – see Fig. 9 (a) and (b).

Curved Lines
On any curved line, be it circle, half-circle, quarter-circle or serpentine, the properly trained, suppled and gymnasticised horse is required to follow, with his hind-feet, exactly the same track on which his fore-feet move. It used to be thought that this achievement was made practicable by causing the entire spine to be uniformly bent, from poll to tail, so as to conform to the degree of curve of the track to be followed. However, recent veterinary research has shown that lateral flexibility is only possible in the forward end of the spine, that is to say forwards from approximately the point on which the rider sits. At that point the flexibility commences gradually and becomes progressively more pronounced through the withers, neck and poll.

To be precise, lateral flexion can be obtained only from the seven cervical (neck) vertebrae and the first thirteen thoracic (dorsal, or back) vertebrae. No measurable lateral flexion can be obtained from the last five thoracic and the contiguous six lumbar vertebrae, nor from the junction of the latter with the entirely rigid pelvis and sacrum. Only the front one-third of the horse's body, excluding the neck, can therefore accommodate itself, and then only to a limited extent, to a curved track. It follows that the rearmost two-thirds of the body must, if the hind-feet remain on the same curved track as the fore-feet, tend to 'cut the corner', just inside the circular track.

This contemporary anatomical discovery severely damages several very longstanding tenets of classical dressage dogma and it may be some time before the theory of how to ride circular or curved tracks is fully adjusted to it. In the meantime, it is probable that the horse's ability to perform a circle, with all four legs following an identical track, must depend very largely upon the looseness of his hip joints and the consequent ability to twist the head of the femur within that joint. The ability of the horse to do this is, however, very limited.

Whatever the degree of severity of the curve or circle on which the horse is travelling, he should always and at all gaits be flexed laterally in the poll, neck and fore-hand to conform as closely as anatomically practicable to the curving track. He must remain in balance throughout the movement, this being correctly demonstrated if the contact with the inside rein is slightly lighter than that on the outside rein while the inside bend is retained. By the same token, the horse must remain obedient to, and not lean against, the rider's inside leg which will be controlling the movement around the curve. There should be no change in tempo or rhythm when the horse moves from a straight line onto a curved one.

Circles

All circles are expected to be ridden on an exactly circular line, the horse exhibiting no inclination either to cut in or to fall out from the regular curve. The rider is also expected to ride the circles at the exact dimensions prescribed in a test for competition. It goes without saying that each circle must be commenced and completed at the precise point in the arena that is stipulated in the test-sheet (see Chapter 9).

It is generally accepted that the smallest circle, or volte, that a horse should, or can reasonably, be asked to perform is one of six metres diameter, sometimes called the academic volte. The actual size of six metres is determined by the fact that it represents (approximately) the smallest circle that a horse can effectively be asked to make *anywhere* in an enclosed riding-hall, *whether on one track or on two*. The horse might therefore be asked to make a pirouette, which is a circle on two tracks with the hind-feet at the centre of the circle, in one of the corners of the hall where it would be enclosed by walls on two sides. In such a case the centre of the circle must be located so as to allow sufficient room for the horse's body, neck and head to pivot round his haunches without risk of his nose hitting the wall. The length of a horse is, for general purposes, regarded as three metres (probably three yards, originally) from nose to tail. The centre of the volte must consequently be three metres from the walls on either side of the corner, giving a radius of three metres and a diameter of six.

The word volte is never used for large circles of, for example, more than ten metres diameter. For international competition purposes, it always means six metres.

Lateral Movements – General Principles
The word lateral is, or can be, applied to any movement in which the rider causes the horse's hindlegs to move on a track that is different from but parallel to the track of the forelegs, even though the two tracks may intentionally overlap (see Shoulder-in and Travers).

Lateral movements are ridden for the following purposes:
(a) To develop the horse's suppleness of muscle, looseness of joint, self-carriage, and, in some cases, collection.
(b) To train and develop the horse's responsiveness and obedience to the aids, more especially to the leg and weight aids.
(c) To display the balance, suppleness, obedience and gymnastic dexterity of the horse, together with the horsemanship of the rider.

The greater the angle at which a lateral movement is ridden, the greater the difficulty for the horse, and consequently also for the rider.

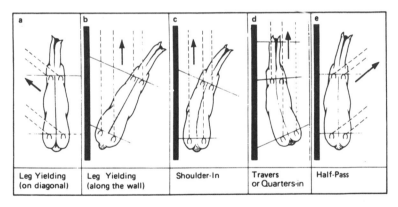

| Leg Yielding (on diagonal) | Leg Yielding (along the wall) | Shoulder-In | Travers or Quarters-in | Half-Pass |

```
- - - - - - - - -  footsteps
————————  angle from track
```
arrow indicates direction of movement

Fig. 20 *Basic lateral movements. (a) Leg-yielding (left). (b) Leg-yielding (left). (c) Shoulder-in (right). (d) Travers or quarters-in (right). (e) Half-pass (right).*

Turn on the Forehand
The turn on the forehand, in which the hindquarters

move around the pivot of the forelegs, is the easiest of all the turns on two tracks that the horse can be asked to perform. With the greater part of his weight placed by nature on his forehand, it is easier for him to move his quarters round the forehand than vice versa. It is also the easiest lesson in aid-obedience for the young horse to understand, since the rider can influence the position of the quarters with his relatively powerful leg aids much more easily than he can influence the forehand. In addition the movement is little more than a sophisticated development of the earliest lesson the young horse learns when he is taught to 'move over' in the stable when being groomed.

When performing a turn on the forehand, the hindlegs have to move around the larger of two concentric circles and have therefore to take longer steps than the forelegs which move around the very small inner circle. It is important that an element of impulsion is maintained throughout, and to ensure that this occurs it becomes vital that the horse's outside hindleg should pass or cross

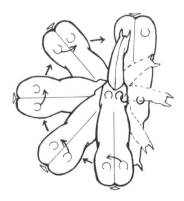

Fig. 21   *Turn on the forehand (right). The inside (right) foreleg forms the pivot of the turn though it should not remain static.*

in front of the inner one. It is insufficient or wrong if the outer leg merely moves up against the inner one and it must never pass behind it. There must never be any sign or tendency to step back with either or any leg. The steps of both front and back legs should be absolutely regular and smoothly placed within the proper walk sequence, the horse remaining quietly and consistently on the bit.

The movement can be performed with the horse quite straight, or he may be flexed or bent to the inside or to the outside according to the wishes of the trainer. More normally, the horse should be slightly bent to the outside so that he looks in the direction in which his head is moving. The real pivot of the movement is the footfall of the foreleg on the side to which the head is moving.

The turn on the forehand is ridden only in the gait of walk. It is rarely used for a turn of more than 180 degrees (half pirouette) though there is no reason why the full circle of 360 degrees should not be ridden.

Turn on the Quarters, or Haunches
The term turn on the haunches is conventionally used to describe a turn in which the forehand is moved around the pivot of the hindlegs at the gait of walk. In fact, the main requirements involved apply equally and exactly to the same type of turn performed in piaffe or in canter (see the Pirouette). Logically, the terms turn on the haunches and pirouette are interchangeable, though the latter name is always used for such a turn in the gait of canter or in piaffe.

The essential factors in a good turn on the haunches in walk are:

(a) The hind-feet, which form the pivot of the turn, should keep moving up and down as part of the normal and absolutely regular four-beat footfall of the gait. The failure of either foot to lift clear of the ground at the appropriate moment constitutes a bad fault, and its

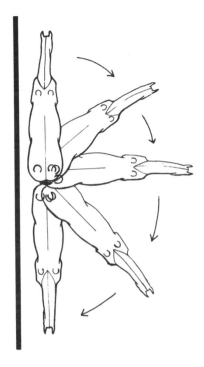

Fig. 22 *Turn on the haunches (or pirouette in walk) (right). The inside hindleg, though maintaining its absolutely regular part in this four-beat gait, forms the pivot of the turn for each step.*

prevention is the rider's chief problem and task. Its accomplishment demands constant forward impulsion combined with longitudinal suppleness and active response to light leg aids. There must, in addition, be no stiffening or resistance in the horse's mouth, poll or neck.

(b) The hindlegs, as the result of constant and lively impulsion, must never show any indication of stepping either outwards or backwards. Every step must be made fractionally but perceptibly forwards and sideways towards the direction of the turn.

(c) The real pivot of the turn is the footfall of the inside hindleg which, ideally, should return to the ground in each step on almost the same spot though moving round a very small circle.

Passada

A passada is an easier, somewhat wider, elongated form of half-turn on the haunches (or half-pirouette). (See Fig. 23.) To begin the movement, the hindlegs move on a quarter circle considerably larger than would be accept-ble in a correct pirouette, the forelegs of course having to go even wider. The passade is completed when the horse is facing in exactly the opposite direction from that in which he began the movement, having passed through 180 degrees and, in doing so, has also steadily made ground to the side for several metres. The forehand must certainly make more ground to the side than the quarters.

At the moment of completion of a passada, the hindlegs and the forelegs should arrive simultaneously on the line of departure, on one track.

The chief factor about a passada is that, to perform it at all, the hindlegs have to make a lot of ground to the side as well as forming a mobile pivot, for the turn of the forehand. The necessity for the horse thus to make this definite lateral movement of the hindlegs makes it easier for the rider to keep them lifting in their appropriate sequence, or to prevent them becoming stuck to the ground and so acting as an undesirable fixed pivot as can so easily happen with true pirouettes. For this reason, the passada is frequently and usefully employed as a training or, equally usefully, as a corrective exercise when the rider has been having difficulty in maintaining the activity of the hindlegs with a more advanced horse. By reverting to the greater mobility of the passada, the horse

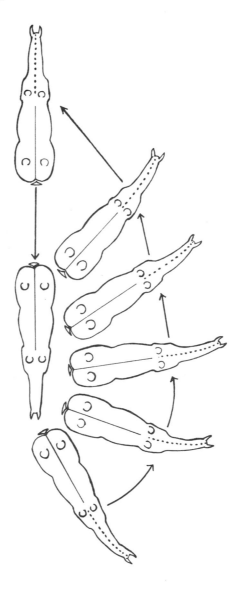

Fig. 23   *The passada. An enlarged and elongated form of turn on the haunches.*

is helped and encouraged to regain the necessary hindleg activity.

Leg-yielding

Leg-yielding (see Fig. 20 (a) and (b)) means, quite simply, that the horse yields to, or obeys, the pressure of the rider's leg acting more or less centrally on his body so that the whole horse, rather than just the hindquarters or the forehand, moves sideways away from the pressure.

Used in a logical training sequence, the horse will first be taught the easiest form of the leg-yielding lesson, ie turning on the forehand, either on the move or on the spot, in which he has to obey or yield to the leg with his quarters only. In that case the rider's leg will be placed comparatively far back from its normal position on the girth. When he has mastered and become accustomed to that method of motion, he can be introduced to the next and rather more difficult lesson of moving his whole body to the side in response to leg-pressure applied less far back. This is the conventional form of leg-yielding.

In the form of leg-yielding that is ridden in competitions, no bend or special degree of collection is demanded, the horse remaining quite straight between poll and tail and with only a slight flexion at the poll itself to the opposite side to the direction of movement. Because no collection or bend is required, all muscles can remain loose, free and unconstrained, with the result that leg-yielding is the easiest and least demanding of all the lateral movements performed on two straight and parallel tracks. It can be performed, as the horse becomes more advanced in its training, in all the three gaits of walk, trot and canter.

In the training programme, leg-yielding can be used as a preliminary exercise to the more difficult (because collected and bent) exercises of shoulder-in and half-pass. It can also be used as a loosening and refreshing exercise in the event of the horse becoming too tied-up and restricted by excessive practice of the half-pass.

Leg-yielding can be used to move on two straight and parallel tracks, but it can also be used at a somewhat later stage of training on circular or curved tracks, either with the quarters in or with quarters out. The circular movements are much more difficult exercises for the horse, but they have their uses at times when the trainer wishes to increase the sideways-moving agility. More usually they are performed on straight, parallel lines and only at a relatively mild angle so as to reduce the risk of the horse striking one leg against the other.

The essence of leg-yielding lies in the straightness of the horse and in the freedom with which the outside fore- and hindlegs cross over the inside limbs. Because the outside hindleg has to cross the line of the body in a somewhat pendulum-like manner which prohibits any extra flexion of the hock (see also shoulder-in), the exercise of leg-yielding can have no collecting effect.

Shoulder-in
The shoulder-in – see Fig. 20 (c) – by far the most important and valuable single exercise in the whole dressage curriculum, is ridden by causing the horse to move with a bend to the inside of his poll, neck and front half of his body (the rear half cannot bend), and by so positioning the forehand that the forelegs move on a track just inside that of the quarters, the latter remaining on their original alignment. The horse looks away from the direction of movement and is driven to the side by the rider's inside leg on the girth.

There can be several degrees of shoulder-in, depending on the suppleness of the horse and the degree to which the rider is able to take the forehand to the inside. In general, however, the movement can be recognised in three phases.

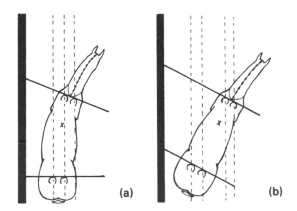

Fig. 24 (a) *Shoulder-in. Correct. Quarters square; three tracks; inside hindleg moves towards centre of gravity (x); inside hock flexes; horse bends round rider's inside leg. See also Fig. 10 (c). (b) Incorrect. Quarters turned; four tracks; inside hindleg not towards centre of gravity (x); inside hindleg stiff (pendulum action) and not flexing; total effect as leg-yielding but with bend.*

First phase: A slight inward bend which will have the effect of bringing the forehand only slightly to the inside to the extent that the outside fore-foot will make a track between the tracks of the two hind-feet, with the inside fore-foot moving well inside the other tracks. There will, in effect, be four separate but overlapping tracks. This form of the movement is usually referred to as Shoulder-fore, a term originally used by the nineteenth-century master Steinbrecht (see Fig. 10 (b)).

Second phase: The full or basic shoulder-in, as recognised today, is a form of the movement in which the bend of the horse is further increased to result in the outside fore-foot moving on exactly the same track as the inside hind-foot. There are three distinct tracks; one for the outside hind-foot; one for the inside hind- and outside fore-foot; and one for the inside fore-foot.

Third phase: This is an exaggerated form of shoulder-in in which the bend of the horse's spine is so marked that the movement is performed on four separate tracks, without any overlapping. However, this four-track form of shoulder-in cannot be produced without sacrificing the squareness of the quarters to the track and, even worse, the vital requirement that the inside hind-foot should move in the direction of the horse's centre of gravity to encourage flexion of the hock (see next paragraph). This consideration is particularly relevant in the light of recent research which has shown that no lateral bend whatever can be made in that part of the horse's spine that lies behind the rider's seat. It is for these reasons that only the three-track form of shoulder-in is required in international competitions, the four-track version being automatically regarded as faulty. For similar reasons it is not practicable to provide a realistic illustration of a four-track shoulder-in without distorting the horse's frame.

The practical purposes and uses of the shoulder-in movement are:

(a) To provide the rider with the ability to place his horse's forehand in front of its quarters, thereby counteracting or curing crookedness.

(b) To stretch and supple the muscles and ligaments of the inside shoulder and forearm, thus increasing the horse's ability to move his forearm gymnastically in any other lateral movement. The shoulder muscles are stretched when the horse has to pass his inside foreleg across and in front of the outside leg.

(c) By moving the forehand somewhat towards the inside of the original track, to cause the inside hindleg to step more towards and under the horse's centre of gravity, which is located just behind the line of the girth, thus causing it to carry additional weight and, in doing so, to increase the strength and flexibility of the hock and the lowering of the quarter. This action, carried out alternately for both hindlegs, constitutes and encourages the beginning of collection (see Fig. 24 (a)).

The greatest weakness of a poor shoulder-in occurs when the horse's forehand and centre of gravity are taken too far to the inside and beyond the line of the track which the inner hindleg is required to follow and when, as a consequence, the quarters have been allowed to turn inwards from their original alignment. When this happens, the inside hind-foot ceases, perforce, to move towards the centre of gravity; will consequently not be carrying extra weight; and will have no need to flex – Fig. 24 (b).

The faulty situation just described is further exacerbated by the following factor. The hind-feet will, if the quarters are turned, be pointing away from their original alignment. But since the hocks can only bend in the direction in which the toes are pointing; and since the toes will no longer be pointing along the original track which the hind-feet must still follow; the hocks will be physically unable to flex, however hard the horse may try. The legs, and particularly the all-important inside hindleg, will have to swing somewhat sideways and stiffly, as they do when leg-yielding. This destroys one of the chief objects of the exercise which then becomes, in the context of collection, virtually valueless – Fig. 24 (b).

With these factors in mind it should become clear that to get the full value and beauty out of the shoulder-in exercise, it should be performed on three tracks, the quarters remaining squarely positioned on their original alignment with the hips virtually at right-angles to the track.

Travers and Renvers
In many respects the travers and renvers movements, both being very nearly identical in their physical demands on the horse, represent the inverse aspects of the

shoulder-in. Whereas in shoulder-in the horse is bent away from the direction of movement, and it is the forehand and forelegs that are repositioned, in travers and renvers the horse is bent and looks towards the direction of movement and it is the hindquarters that have to be repositioned in their relation to the forehand

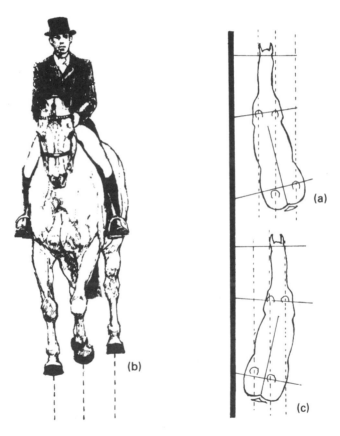

Fig. 25 *Travers and renvers. (a) Travers (right) – forehand on original track; quarters on inner track; three tracks; horse bent round rider's inside (right) leg. (b) Travers (left). (c) Renvers (left) – quarters (hind-feet) on original track; forehand on inner track; three tracks; horse bent round rider's inside (left) leg.*

(see Fig. 25). All three movements should be ridden on a three-track basis and can be performed anywhere, along the wall, on the centre-line or on any imaginary curved or straight track.

In the travers, the horse's head and forehand remain on the original track or line of movement, but the

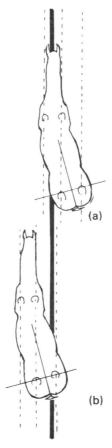

Fig. 26 *Travers and renvers on centre line. (a) Travers (right) – forehand on main track. (b) Renvers (right) – quarters on main track. Note: This distinction may be required as a test of accurate riding in competitions.*

quarters are brought to the inside (assuming the movement to be performed along the wall or boards of an
arena) so that the horse moves on three tracks with the
outside hind-foot following the same track as the inside
fore-foot. The degree of bend within the neck should
conform to the bend achieved within the forehand,
bearing in mind that any spinal bend can only commence
at midspine.

In the renvers, the horse moves and is bent in exactly
the same manner as in travers, but in this case his hind-
feet follow the original track while his fore-feet follow a
parallel line. As with the shoulder-in and travers, three
tracks should be shown. Thus, the only difference
between travers and renvers concerns the question of
whether the forehand or the hindquarters are on the
original track. The one is no more difficult for the horse
than the other, except in the early stages of training when
the controlling presence of the wall will make the travers
somewhat easier, and it is for that reason that it is usually
introduced first. When the two movements are both
required in the same competition test, it is done to test
the rider's ability to place and maintain his horse in
different though related positions irrespective of any
assistance provided by the wall or boards, or of the
horse's tendency to recognise and follow a track with his
eyes. At an advanced stage, travers and renvers can be
ridden on the centre line of an arena, the difference in
that circumstance being illustrated in Fig. 26.

From the very beginning of training it is always easier
to shift or reposition the horse's quarters than his
forehand, as for example when teaching the earliest of all
lateral movements – the turn on the forehand. It is for
this reason that travers/renvers is a much easier movement to ride than the shoulder-in which requires the
repositioning of the forehand. In addition, and because
in travers the horse continues to look precisely where he

is going, the rider has to make much less use of the reins and can rely much more on the use of his seat and legs to produce the required bend and alignment. There is consequently less risk of disturbance to the horse's mouth and to his impulsion.

On the other hand, and due to the fact that in travers the quarters are of necessity swung away from the original or main line of progression, they will be more or less forced to function as in leg-yielding and the movement will consequently have little or no collection effect (see shoulder-in for the converse). Impulsion through the horse may also suffer because the horse will be, in effect, crooked.

The chief uses for these two exercises are to improve the mobility and obedience of the quarters to the rider's outside leg; to stretch, loosen and free the muscles and ligaments of the quarters and, in particular, of the hip-joints; and, because there will be hardly any bend at the poll and a nearly even contact with both reins, to improve and establish the freedom of the gaits in lateral work.

Travers and renvers can be ridden in all three gaits, on straight lines or on curved and circular lines. When the renvers is ridden on curved lines, and because the hindlegs will then be moving on the outside or longer track, the horse will try to place more weight on his forehand in his efforts to assist his hindlegs to make the longer steps. Conversely, when the travers is ridden on a circle, it will have the effect of making the horse place more weight on his quarters in his effort to lighten the forehand to facilitate the longer steps then required of the forelegs as they move around the outer and longer track.

The travers is also, and perhaps more logically, referred to as the Quarters-in, and the renvers as Quarters-out. The use of this nomenclature is more readily intelligible to students and beginners, and also obviates the question of whether, as is so often claimed, the travers is merely a variation of the half-pass, or vice versa, the latter being also sometimes called a Traversalle (across the hall). There are strong arguments to suggest that there are fundamental differences between the two, as will be discussed below under the heading of The Half-pass.

The Half-pass

The half-pass is perhaps the ultimate, the most impressive and the most dignified of all the lateral movements. When executed accurately and well, it demonstrates in a striking manner the rider's control of his horse and the horse's gymnastic ability. It can be performed in walk, trot, canter and passage. As well as on straight lines it can also be performed on a circle in which form it ultimately, when the circle is reduced to minimal proportions, becomes a pirouette.

The half-pass requires the horse to move in a direction diagonal to the alignment of his body. His poll, neck and forehand should be only slightly bent in the direction of the movement. The quality, rhythm and cadence of the gait should remain as good as it was when the horse was moving straight on one track.

A major problem that arises in riding the half-pass is the maintenance of impulsion, that is to say the degree of energy that passes through the back, neck, poll and mouth into the rider's hands. This difficulty, inherent in the mechanics of the movement, is due to two factors which apply to the half-pass more than to any other lateral movement. They are:

(a) The direction of the horse's bodily alignment, and therefore of the flow of impulsion, does not coincide with the direction of actual movement – see Fig. 20 (e). It becomes very difficult for the rider to combine the aids for active, flowing movement in a sideways or diagonal direction with those for active impulsion that must, per

Fig. 27 *The half-pass (left, at trot). The horse, without changing his alignment, moves diagonally to one side. (a) The poll, neck and forehand are slightly bent, in the direction of the movement, around the rider's inside leg, which maintains overall control. (b) The horse's body is straight between saddle and tail.*

se, flow in a significantly different direction. Yet if the impulsion diminishes appreciably, the beauty of the movement is lost, the rhythm will falter, and the horse will become effectively behind the bit.

(b) Because the horse is moving laterally on two quite widely separated tracks, the two hindlegs have to move on precisely parallel lines in a direction that is not the same as the direction of impulsion (straight through the body). They are concerned with propelling the body more or less sideways to the detriment of their ability to push the impulsion forwards. Neither hindleg can therefore be directed towards the horse's centre of gravity and neither, consequently, is asked to carry additional weight. Neither moves in the direction in which the toe is pointing. In short, they have to move, just as they do in leg-yielding, in a manner that does nothing to increase the loading or the flexion of the hocks. It is consequently difficult to keep the hindlegs properly engaged, more particularly the inside one which may tend to dwell too far behind due to any lack of proper stimulation by the rider's inside leg which is also concerned with maintaining the bend in the area of the girth. That double role of the inside leg is not the least of the rider's problems.

Nevertheless, and despite all these considerable difficulties, it is clear that if the horse is ridden in half-pass along a consistent diagonal line from one prescribed point to another, all his four legs must travel along exactly parallel lines and not, as has sometimes been written, with the inside hindleg being engaged more forward and less sideways than the outside one. If it did that, the horse would not arrive in one piece at the end, and the track-lines would get tangled up instead of remaining tidily parallel, as they must and in practice do.

With the exception of one factor, the position of shoulder-in is the ideal position from which to commence a half-pass, ie to move from right shoulder-in into right half-pass. The one exception is that the half-pass is required to have a lesser bend in the neck and forehand than the shoulder-in and the rider must therefore take appropriate steps to adjust the degree of bend as he makes the transition from the latter movement into the former, or vice versa.

The sideways movement of a half-pass in canter and in trot is created almost entirely by the action, or thrust, of the horse's outside hindleg. None of the other three legs is able to exert any appreciable thrust to the side.

Counter Changes of Hand

Theoretically, this term could mean any quick or sudden change of direction, as when a horse is caused to move on a zig-zag course. In practice, in strict dressage parlance, a counter change of hand means, quite specifically, a change from a half-pass in one direction to a half-pass in the opposite direction. In competitions the movement is frequently required to be ridden in a series of a specified number of counter changes, usually three or five, on a zig-zag course from one side of the centre line to the other.

When ridden in trot gait, the distance to which the horse is required to travel from the centre line is always specified in metres. When ridden in canter, the number of strides on each side of the line is specified. The length of each leg of the zig-zag, especially when measured in strides for the canter, is expected to be performed with meticulous accuracy.

The half-passes themselves should be executed in exactly the same manner in every detail as the ordinary form of half-pass. This applies to the collection, the bend, the rhythm, the cadence, the lightness and to all other characteristics of true lateral movement.

The actual counter change refers to the point or

moment at which the direction changes. It will be seen in Fig. 28 that there will always be one more leg or track to be covered than the number of counter changes of hand. For example, there are four separate legs in a sequence of three counter changes, and six separate legs in a sequence of five counter changes.

The horse must not only be appropriately bent in each of the half-passes, he must also be shown to be absolutely straight for an instant before starting the new direction. And, as in the half-pass, in each leg of the movement the forehand should be fractionally ahead of the quarters.

The counter change in canter necessitates a flying change of leg (see below) at the end of each half-pass, so as to enable the horse to canter correctly in the new direction. The flying change must be made immediately after the last of the strides specified for each half-pass. The landing of the horse from the flying change has to count as the first stride in the new half-pass. The simultaneous change of bend and canter lead, performed in perfect balance and preceded by absolute straightness, poses considerable difficulties for the rider.

Flying Change of Leg

In order to change the leading leg in a canter, eg from canter left to canter right, without breaking into a trot or walk during the process, the horse has at some point to readjust his entire sequence of footfall. A subtle but definite change has to be made to the action of all four legs at very nearly the same instant, and this is only possible during the very brief moment when all four legs are off the ground at the same time, ie during the moment of complete suspension that follows the third beat of the canter, the beat when the leading foreleg is alone on the ground. This mid-air reorganisation is called a flying change of leg. Suddenly, but without any jerk or disturbance of balance or rhythm, the horse will be

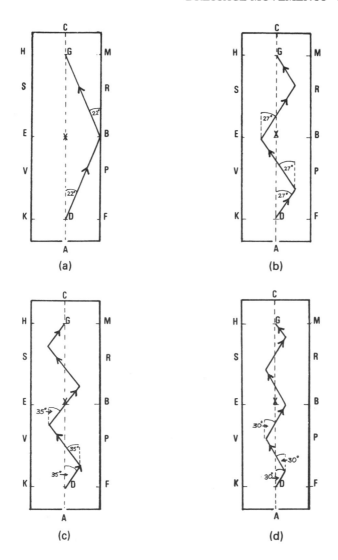

Fig. 28   *Counter changes of hand. (a) One counter change of hand (at B) – 10m to each side. (b) Three counter changes of hand – four canter strides to each side of centre line. (c) Four counter changes of hand – four canter strides to each side of centre line. (d) Five counter changes of hand – three strides to each side of centre line.*

cantering on the other leg.

With a well-trained horse and a skilful rider, the flying change of lead can be effected with great frequency according to the rider's wish or whim, perhaps every fourth stride, perhaps every second stride, or even every single stride. A sequence of fifteen flying changes at every stride constitutes a very advanced feat of horsemanship and equine skill, in the course of which it will be seen that the horse, while maintaining forward fluency, impulsion and rhythm, never makes two consecutive strides on the same lead. This feat, to be good, should look perfectly easy for both horse and rider as if it required no special effort by either. The rider's aids should, as always, be almost invisible.

Fifteen is the maximum number of one-time flying changes that may be expected in Grand Prix competition, if only for reasons of limited space in the arena. But very much larger numbers are sometimes performed without breaking the sequence by very talented riders with exceptional horses. Two or three hundred at a time have been achieved.

The alteration of sequence of footfall required of the horse involves primarily a quick adjustment of one hindleg in exactly the same manner as a child changes its footfall from the normal when skipping along a pavement, while holding onto mother's hand, or even without that comforting aid. To do this, the child puts the same foot to the ground twice in succession. Instead of treading right-left-right, as in normal stepping, the child steps right-right-left, or left-left-right, and because a small jump is essential to make this change practicable, the child will now be running instead of walking. The horse likewise cannot change his leg sequence from a walk.

For the horse, the technique is essentially the same as it is for the child. The canter left, for example, is initiated by the right hindleg – Fig. 29 (a); the left hindleg then

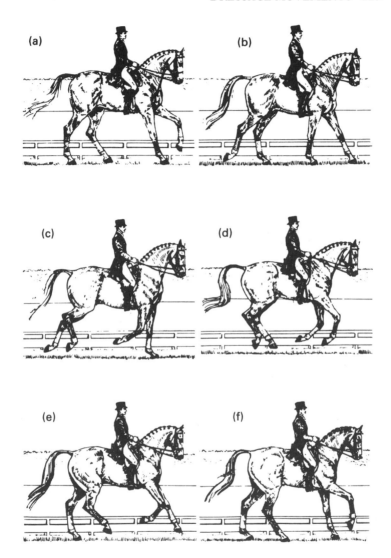

Fig. 29 *Flying changes of leg in canter. (a) The canter left begins with thrust from right hindleg. (b) Progresses. (c) Canter left complete. (d) In suspension – change taking place. (e) The canter right begins with thrust from left hindleg. (f) Progresses and completes followed by suspension.*

DRESSAGE

Fig. 30 *A firm and influential seat is needed by the rider during a flying change. The pelvis slightly leads the torso and shoulders to retain control throughout.*

follows as part of the second beat in exact conjunction with the right foreleg; and finally the left or leading foreleg comes to the ground while the other three are progressively coming off it. Then, during the period of total suspension that occurs after the leading foreleg has done its work, and in order to make a flying change into the canter right, the horse has to expedite the forward movement of the left hindleg so that it catches up and passes in front of the right hindleg which has hitherto preceded it, while the latter is still in the air (Fig. 29 (e)). The left hindleg thus comes to the ground first, to initiate the next stride which will consequently be in the new canter right, the forelegs quite naturally taking their cue from the hindlegs. The flying change has been accomplished.

A good flying change should flow absolutely smoothly from one lead to the other, with no pause or loss of impulsion and with no sign of hesitation or loss of balance. The horse should appear to make the change with pride, elegance and complete confidence. It then becomes only a matter of practice and experience, with improving balance and gymnastic freedom of movement, to master eventually the technique of making changes with increasing frequency.

But it is by no means only the horse that has a difficult task in becoming totally proficient in flying changes. Very considerable skill and sense of timing have to be developed by the rider if he is to execute sequence changes without detriment to his own balance, relaxation and independence of aids. Any weakness of that kind in the riding will immediately be reflected in the performance of the horse.

It is important, if the flying change is to be impressive and good, that the length of the actual stride in which the change takes place should be at least as long, and perhaps a trifle longer, than the strides that precede and follow it. There must be no shortening and no dwelling.

To achieve flying changes that are fluent, balanced, generous and straight, and to do so consistently, the rider must keep his seat firmly in the saddle, and his body in balance above it, so that he can influence and push through the movement with his pelvis without disturbing the horse.

The Schaukel
Schaukel is a German word meaning a see-saw or rocker. It is used in dressage as the name for a movement in

which the horse is required to step alternately backwards and forwards for a few usually prescribed number of steps in each direction, but without actually halting before the change of direction. The number of steps called for is not necessarily the same for the forward as for the backward movement, and may vary between three and six for competition purposes and according to the standard of severity of the test. The horse walks forward in the correct four-beat sequence of that gait and reins-back in more or less accurate two-time sequence as already described for the ordinary rein-back. (See page 93.)

There should be no measurable pause between the two opposed movements, the leg or foot that moved last in one direction being the first to move, before it has been firmly grounded or taken any weight, in the opposite direction.

The shaukel usually terminates with a rein-back, after which the horse is expected to go forward again promptly and directly into whichever of the three basic gaits is requested, with no intermediate steps if the trot or canter is called for.

The Pirouette

The pirouette is, in dressage, one complete turn on the haunches of 360 degrees. It can be performed at the walk, the canter and the piaffe, but each of them in a highly collected form. The trot gait is not applicable because it essentially involves positive forward movement. But the trot becomes a piaffe when the two-beat gait is used on, or almost on, the spot; hence the practicability of pirouetting in piaffe.

In whichever gait the pirouette is performed, it is a prime requirement that the rhythm, tempo, balance and cadence of the gait should remain the same throughout the turn as they were during the approach. They should also remain unchanged during the exit from the turn. It is the difficulty of maintaining the lively activity of the hindlegs, essential to the rhythm and proper sequence of footfall without significant forward movement, that makes the pirouette possibly the most difficult of all dressage movements to execute successfully. Under no circumstances should the horse tend, or appear, to move backwards during the movement, even in the slightest degree.

It helps to understand the technicalities of the pirouette if it is appreciated that it is in effect only a half-pass executed on a minimal circle, ie a circle with a diameter of the length of the horse measured between its front and back feet. Within that limitation, all the normal requirements of the half-pass pertain, including especially a slight bend to the inside through the forehand, neck and poll. It is also essential that the quarters are not allowed to fall outwards, against the rider's controlling leg.

Pirouette in Walk This is the form of pirouette in which the horse is most likely to lose the rhythm of the gait in his hind-feet to the extent that one hind-foot may swivel round without lifting off the ground at all. The problem for the rider is to maintain sufficient impulsion with a corresponding soft submission and acceptance of the bit.

In a walk pirouette, with its unbroken and continuous four-beat sequence of footfall, it is the inside hindleg that forms the main pivot of the circle. It remains nearest to the centre and the others move around it.

Pirouette in Canter This form of pirouette makes the greatest demands on the overall gymnastic ability and balance of the horse and on the sensitivity and horseman-ship of the rider. To keep up a canter of maximum collection with its correct three-beat sequence, through-

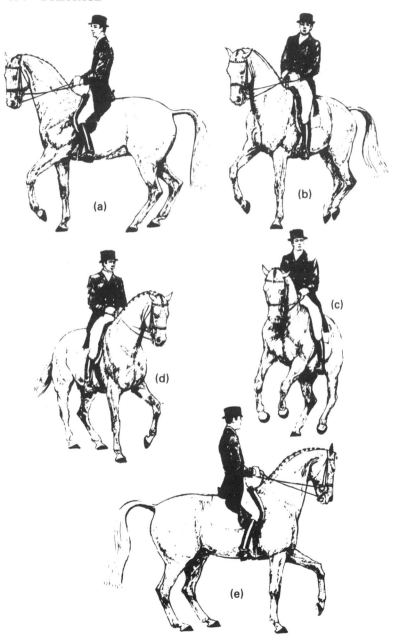

Fig. 31 *The pirouette. (a) Pirouette begins – horse collected; gesetzen and flexed. (b) Outside hindleg coming to the ground to create the next turn. (c) Outside hindleg creates the turn of which it forms the pivot. (d) Second beat of canter stride, as in (a). (e) Half-pirouette completed. (f) The turn progresses. (g) Turning, still in maximum collection. (h) Pirouette (360°) completed. Horse exits forward in original direction, still in collection and perfect control.*

out a 360-degree turn in which the hind-feet move round an area no bigger than a plate, presents the horse with a problem of the highest degree of difficulty. That degree of difficulty is, of course, shared with the rider/trainer.

When executing the pirouette correctly, the horse will be seen to adopt a posture in which his quarters are lowered and engaged under his mass to the extent that he will appear to be somewhat sitting-down (*gesetzen*, in German phraseology). Only in this way is he able to solve his two main problems which are:

(a) To make the small jump that is an integral and essential part of every canter-stride, but in this case without moving significantly forward.

(b) To so lighten his forehand that he can bring it round the perimeter of the circle, taking much longer steps than the hindlegs which only have to move round the very much smaller inner circle, but without losing the vital three-beat sequence in which the inside hind- and outside fore-feet come to the ground at virtually the same moment. Very great muscular strength and activity in the loins and quarters are required and yet the horse must never be allowed to hurry either the rhythm or the turn itself. He should appear to wait upon the rider's inside leg which allows him to make each successive turn of approximately 50 degrees.

If the canter is insufficiently collected, and the forehand insufficiently lightened, the horse will have no option but to lift the forehand round by an unharmonious heave of his loins for each successive segment of the turn. When this happens, the fore-feet will both be above the ground for much longer than the hind-feet and the diagonal beat will be non-existent. The canter will be badly flawed and the pirouette unworthy of its name.

In the correct canter pirouette, with its series of independent canter-leaps, each of which comprises an element of half-pass, it is the outside hindleg that forms the pivot of each successive segment of the turn as it comes to the ground, before the others, after each successive moment of suspension. It performs this thrust to the side in exactly the same manner as it does in a normal canter half-pass. A full pirouette of 360 degrees should be completed in six or eight jump-turns. The horse will therefore have to turn himself on that outside hindleg approximately 50 degrees with each canter stride.

Pirouette in Piaffe This form of pirouette is not as difficult as it may sound, assuming of course that the basic form of piaffe has already been fully mastered. Once the piaffe has been sufficiently developed so that it can be performed for quite a prolonged period with plenty of activity, submission, impulsion and balance, very little extra difficulty is involved when the rider quietly leads the horse round, little step by little step, into the pirouette turn while carefully controlling the quarters. The fact that the piaffe, to be performed at all, necessitates a very high degree of collection results in there being less tendency for the horse to let his quarters swing outwards or to become inactive, or for the horse to turn himself on his centre, two things that he is liable to do in either the walk or the canter form of this fascinating and beautiful movement.

In addition, and in contrast to the pirouette in canter, the haunches in the piaffe continue to carry their high proportion of weight in an unbroken manner throughout the whole turn. In the canter pirouette, on the other hand, there is a moment in each and every one of the six or eight strides required to complete the circle when all the weight of the horse is of necessity carried only by the leading foreleg. From the easier and more consistent balance of the piaffe, as compared with the canter, the horse will feel less hurried and under less strain. Consequently he will remain more calm.

Piaffe

The French verb *piaffer* translates rather uncomfortably into English as to prance, or paw the ground. One can see what was meant in the first place, but neither alternative bears much relation to the movement we know as the classical equestrian piaffe.

The movement or air of piaffe represents the ultimate in collected mobility, the horse carrying a very large proportion of his weight on his quarters and, when the movement is well executed, showing great freedom and elevation of the shoulders and forelegs. The horse should, accordingly, be very light and submissive in hand though clearly maintaining forward impulsion. Some limited but actual forward movement is acceptable, and indeed necessary in the early stages of training, but in its full fruition the piaffe has to be performed exactly (or almost exactly) on the spot. But nonetheless and above all, there must never be any indication of a backward-moving tendency, even by one leg, and there should be no swaying from side to side or crossing of the legs. The horse must remain straight and forward in body and in the action of his limbs.

The piaffe should always be executed in a perfect two-time gait sequence with a clear moment of suspension between the two beats. However, the period in suspension will be less than in any other form of trot.

The piaffe is commonly referred to as a form of trot on the spot, albeit very highly collected, cadenced and elevated. But it can also be regarded, with perhaps a greater accuracy, as being more closely related to the passage, an air which shares with the piaffe all the qualities just mentioned and, in particular, the slow, cadenced and majestic rhythm, despite the fact that the passage involves steady and unhurried progress forward (see below under Passage). The similarity between piaffe and passage is most strikingly seen when, fully trained,

Fig. 32   *The piaffe – a kind of trot (or passage) on the spot. Maximum collection and engagement of the lowered quarters; activity of the hindlegs; lightness of the forehand; proud submission.*

the horse can demonstrate the transition from the one air to the other without any visible change or alteration of the rhythm or cadence.

Steady and unhurried rhythm and cadence, together with a supple, swinging back and submissive mouth, are of greater importance than the elevation or height to which the feet are lifted. The ideal piaffe, however, requires the fore-feet to be raised in turn to halfway between the fetlock and the knee of the opposite leg, and the hind-feet to just above the fetlock. Only a small minority of horses are sufficiently talented to reach that ideal while maintaining all the other desired qualities already mentioned. To achieve the required collection and balance, the quarters must be well lowered which, with a supple and swinging back, will bring the head into a vertical position.

The Passage

The meaning of the French word *passage*, derived from the Latin *passagio*, appears to have no recognisable connection with the dressage movement that now carries it as its label. The best that can be said is that the word carries connotations in connection with step, or stepping, deriving from the French *pas*, a step. A passage is certainly a notably fine-stepping and measured form of progression. In practice, however, there is nothing obscure or complicated about the passage which is perhaps the most easily and unmistakeably recognisable of all the school movements.

The passage is a form of trot, at least insofar as it cannot be performed in any of the other gait sequences. It has, like the trot itself and the piaffe, a precise and absolutely equal two-time diagonal footfall, but it is a trot with an exceptional degree of collection, a exceptional degree of cadence, and an exceptional degree of elevation. The last two of those three factors would not be possible

Fig. 33 *Passage. (a) Right diagonal in suspension with excellent elevation. (b) Full suspension. (c) Left diagonal in suspension. Note: the horse remains more horizontal than in piaffe, making slow but stately progress forward with maximum period of suspension between steps.*

without the first. From that collection the horse is able to direct the greater part of his power upwards rather than forwards, which accounts for and produces the elevation and the relative slowness of the tempo and speed, compared with the normal collected trot. Because of the increased upward thrust, there is a prolonged period of time in suspension. There is no element of hesitancy as is sometimes suggested by people who have not studied the subject, the legs and feet moving continuously and at a constant speed along the arc of their course through the air until they once more come to the ground.

The elevation of the fore- and hind-feet should, ideally, correspond with the elevation required in piaffe as described above. The two airs are therefore very closely akin, the chief distinction lying in the fact that the passage, which has to make significant forward progress, requires a greater proportion of the horse's energy to be directed into a moderately forward thrust. Since the essence and spirit of the movement lies in its elevation, the rate of speed of forward progress should be very modest. The horse's body will be nearer the horizontal in passage, with a more nearly equal loading of the four legs. It would be a mistake, however, to think that the piaffe requires a noticably lower degree of impulsion.

A horse that performs both piaffe and passage with ease, pride, lightness, freedom and perfect regularity, and can move from one into the other without noticeable effort or disturbance, is demonstrating the very quintessence of good dressage, and the rider the quintessence of artistic presentation.

7: Arenas

Dressage, for training or display purposes, can take place or be practised anywhere; indoors, outdoors, in wide spaces or in restricted areas. For competition purposes, it has to be staged, either indoors or outdoors, in an arena of prescribed size and description.

But wherever or for whatever purpose it is practised, there are certain qualities of underfoot-surface that must essentially exist if any serious purpose is to be served. These qualities are:

(a) The area to be ridden on must be flat, though not necessarily absolutely horizontal. Any relatively slight slope that may exist should be continuous and uniform.

(b) The surface of the arena must be smooth enough not to cause discomfort or bruising to the soles of the horse's feet, nor to cause him to stumble, or to affect his confidence.

(c) The condition of the ground or surface, together with the undersurface, must be firm but not slippery; not deep, so that the horse has difficulty in moving his feet; and not so hard that it will jar or damage the horse's legs. There should always be a degree of resilience in the surface that will receive but support the very considerable weight imposed by the steps of a horse weighing between ten and fifteen hundredweight.

Grass areas
When in perfect condition, with a thick carpet of grass on dry, light and well-drained soil, a grass riding area can hardly be bettered. Unfortunately the grass very soon

becomes worn if many horses are worked on the same area, and a heavy shower of rain may make it temporarily slippery. Depending on the subsoil, very heavy rain may quickly turn the whole site into a quagmire in which no horse can function effectively. For these reasons, grass competition arenas, though quite normal twenty years ago for even the highest levels of international dressage, are no longer considered sufficiently reliable for important competitions. They are now specifically excluded from use in an Olympic Games.

All-weather surfaces
Twenty or thirty years ago, when all-weather surfaces first became popular for outdoor work, they were usually constructed of sand. Now, in the eighties, they are made of many kinds or mixtures of materials, always in the search for a firm, resilient, stable surface that will remain unaffected by rain-storms. Because all-weather areas tend, by their nature, to be permanent fixtures, great attention has to be given to the provision of good foundations as well as to the problem of drainage and water-disposal. The foundation is particularly important when there is a clay top-soil or sub-soil. A good all-weather arena is invariably very expensive to construct and mistakes or failures in construction are likely to be very costly matters.

Competition arenas
Competition arenas are always, by long tradition, in one of two sizes.
Full size . . . . . . 20 metres x 60 metres
Small size . . . . . . 20 metres x 40 metres
All international competitions, and most national competitions at advanced level, are ridden in the full-sized arena.
All arenas should invariably be completely surrounded

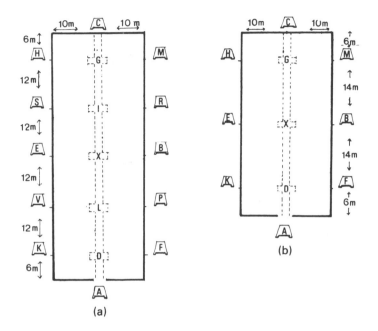

Fig. 34   *Arenas. (a) Full size, 20m x 60m. (b) Small size, 20m x 40m.*
Note: Letters on the centre line are notional.

by a wall or by low fencing or boards, within which boundaries all the movements required in a test must be performed.

Arena lettering

A standard pattern of lettering is used to mark certain positions in all arenas, these letters acting as points of reference for defining the various movements that the rider is required to execute (see Fig. 34). In addition to the twelve letters that mark positions around the perimeter, another five letters denote equivalent points on the centre line, the line that joins the centre points of the two short ends of the arena. These centre-line letters are in practice only notional, since the whole of the arena

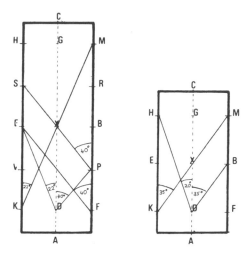

Fig. 35   *Arena angle. Degrees of difficulty in lateral movements – the greater the angle the greater the difficulty.*

floor has to be kept clear to allow unobstructed movement by the horses.

The system or arrangement of the lettering, though not entirely logical, is internationally accepted and never varies. Its origins remain obscure.

Ideally the centre line, together with its letter points, should be indicated on the arena surface by close mowing on grass or by heavy rolling on sand or other all-weather surfaces. With the latter type of arena, the surface is usually raked and the centre line re-rolled after every five or six competitors.

If a horse leaves the arena with all four feet, at any time between his entry and the completion of the test, he will be eliminated.

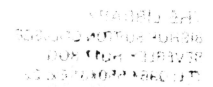

8: Competitions and Contests

A dressage *Competition* comprises a gathering of competitors for the purpose of taking part in one or several different *Contests* at various levels, the whole programme often being spread over several days. A *Test* is the actual programme or sequence of movements that the competitor has to execute in the arena for each contest.

All contests fall into one of two categories, either:

(a) *A prescribed test* which lays down in detail the movements to be ridden; the precise route to be followed, including the points of commencement and ending; and where and for what particular qualities the marks should be given by the judge.

(b) *Free-style contests*, or *Kürs*, for which each competitor devises his own programme which has to include certain specified movements, according to the standard of the contest, and has to be completed within a specified time that will be checked by a stop-watch. In this style of contest, marks are allocated by the judges for each specified movement as and when it is shown, and which, added up, form the basis for one single mark for technical merit. An additional mark (out of ten) is given for the degree of difficulty of the programme shown, and a third mark for the overall artistic merit and impression. The latter mark is particularly relevant with the Kürs is ridden to music.

The great majority of contests fall into category (a) (prescribed tests) which includes tests for all the recognised grades of training. National authorities usually provide a choice of several tests within each training grade. The international authorities are concerned only with Advanced training grade and provide a single official test for each of the five subdivisions recognised for international competition.

National Training Grades
Training grades recognised by the British Horse Society are, in ascending order of difficulty or achievement:
Preliminary
Novice
Elementary
Medium
Advanced (including the official international tests – see below)

International Training or Competition Grades
The official international tests, in ascending order of difficulty, are:
The Prix St Georges
The Intermediate 1
The Intermediate 2
The Grand Prix (the regular Olympic test)
The Grand Prix Special (shorter and more difficult than the Grand Prix, used only in addition to the latter, and usually restricted to the top twelve competitors in the Grand Prix)
Note: An International Kür may be set at any of these levels, but is usually at Grand Prix standard.

As a rule, in any major competition a competitor may enter a horse for two contests only, exclusive of the Kür, provided they are either the Prix St Georges and the Intermediate 1; the Intermediate 1 and the Intermediate 2; or the Intermediate 2 and the Grand Prix.
The official international tests, usually reviewed or changed every four years, are used without discrimina-

tion or any form of adjustment for all forms of international competitions including Continental or World Championships and the Olympic Games.

Detailed rules governing permissible dress, saddlery, bridles, bits, behaviour and many other ancillary matters are provided and published by the International Equestrian Federation (FEI) and these are adhered to, with minimal adjustment for special national circumstances, by each National Federation. The FEI Rules are themselves adjusted or amended from time to time, as may be thought necessary and desirable by the governing body of the FEI Dressage Bureau.

9: Judges and Judging

A dressage competition, unlike a dressage display, has to be judged in order to discover the winner and to place the remaining competitors in their appropriate order. But ever since competition dressage first became popular around the turn of the century, judging dressage has been a matter of considerable controversy and has presented many grave problems. These difficulties arise from certain factors inherent in dressage itself but which do not exist in most other sports with the exception of skating and gymnastics. These difficulty-factors are:

(a) So many different but complementary qualities have to be considered, as discussed in Chapters 4, 5 and 6 of this book, throughout the entire performance of each and every movement of every horse, that any hard-and-fast assessment, adjudged on a matter of fact, becomes virtually impossible. With so many qualities, all varying in degree from very poor to very good (see paragraphs on mark valuations below), and all constantly changing as the horse progresses from one movement to another of greater or lesser difficulty, and with the need to commit himself to some numerical decision approximately every twenty seconds, the judge can only hope to reach a reasonably satisfactory compromise within the guidelines worked out and stipulated by the appropriate international authorities. Psychologists tell us that the human brain is capable of dealing with no more than three separate factors at a time, and yet the dressage kaleidoscope presents the judge with many more than that, so it is clear that some of the factors are bound to be given somewhat less than full attention. And furthermore, different judges operating in consort are likely to concentrate on a different selection from the many possible aspects of the picture in front of their eyes.

(b) With so much depending upon personal judgement as opposed to hard fact, it is rare that any two judges will entirely agree on the exact marks deserved by all, or even any, of the twenty, thirty or perhaps forty horses presented to them. There may well be close agreement in regard to a few of the movements, but as the component parts of the test progress, minor mark discrepancies are bound to show up to the extent that even the overall placing of a horse is quite likely to be affected within one or two places, and sometimes many more, as between the assessments of several judges.

(c) An artistic element has always been recognised as an integral part of good dressage. But art is never quantifiable, nor is it ever appreciated on equal terms by any two people. The greater the art in any form, the more impossible it is to assess the artists in terms of marks, and that is as true in dressage-riding as it is in painting, music, sculpture or wine. The artistic element in dressage must certainly be considered by each of the judges all the time, but it is as likely to be the cause of discrepancy as it is of agreement in the marks allocated by each of several judges. In the end, it is the craftsmanship in dressage that has the main influence on the assessment and marking since it is the only factor that can be specifically defined. Possibly no great harm or loss is caused by that, since true artists are rare in any sphere and dressage riders are no exception.

Over the last three quarters of a century, experiments have been made to discover the number of judges in a panel most likely to produce satisfactory and acceptable results in international competitions, always with a view to minimising the risk of gross discrepancies due to personal bias, chauvinism, or plain human weakness. At the present time, and for a number of years past, reasonably happy results are being obtained by the use of five judges for all major international or national contests, all of them working entirely independently of the others. Their five scores are added together to produce the final score for each horse.

The five judges, though on occasion there may only be three, are always located at standard positions around the arena (see Fig. 35) so that between them they will be able to see most aspects of the competitor's performance. Inevitably, and indeed intentionally, they will not all obtain the same view, some for example seeing the horse in piaffe from the front or the rear while others see it from the side. This is undoubtedly a good thing, but it is another factor that tends to produce discrepancies in the marks.

Marks

A dressage judge, whether working alone (in a national contest) or as one of a panel, is required to allot a mark, out of a maximum of ten, for every movement or closely related small group of movements. The test-sheet will always show where each mark has to be given and what movement or group of movements it relates to. Thus each of five judges will always be making the same number of mark-assessments and for exactly the same range of movements.

The value of each movement performed in a test is evaluated according to the following mark-scale and its verbal equivalent:

10 = Excellent (this does not imply perfection)
9 = Very good
8 = Good
7 = Fairly good
6 = Satisfactory

5 = Sufficient
4 = Insufficient
3 = Fairly bad
2 = Very bad
1 = Not executed

Each mark allotted, preferably together with a brief explanatory comment, has to be spoken aloud, so that both mark and comment can be written down on the sheet by the judge's writer, immediately after the end of the movement. The judge can thus give his entire attention to the next and immediately following movement. The time factor for the judge's mental process of viewing, considering, assessing and marking is extremely short, probably about twenty seconds, and as the process may be more or less continuous for many hours, the judges work under very considerable pressure.

The factors which primarily influence a judge's assessment, apart from obvious mistakes or failures to perform the required movement efficiently as and where demanded, are:

(a) Fluency and freedom of the gait or paces, with regular and unhurried rhythm.

(b) Straightness and impulsion, the hindlegs moving in exactly the same tracks as the forelegs except when performing lateral movements.

(c) Suppleness of the back, allowing muscular activity from the quarters to flow uninterruptedly through the whole horse.

(d) Lightness, which implies balance and dexterity resulting from active engagement of the hindlegs and overall harmony of movement.

(e) Submission, implying a willing and happy cooperation by the horse with the demands from the rider, together with complete absence of muscular resistance. The rider will then appear to direct and control his horse without visible effort, keeping him straight on straight lines and bent appropriately on curved lines and in lateral movements. The horse will appear to accept the aids and controls without fuss and will give the impression of doing of his own accord whatever is required of him.

To judge efficiently, the judge must know by heart the complete test, and he must also memorise, to avoid frequent reference to the test-sheet, the points at which each mark must be given. He must know and understand the principles of classic dressage training and riding; he must never take his eyes from the horse and rider in the arena; and he must be capable of maintaining intense concentration on his task for long spells broken only by a few short breaks in the course of the contest when the arena is raked.

A good judge, in addition to being knowledgable on his subject, must be of impeccable integrity and be capable of excluding from his mind any form of bias towards or against individual horses or riders. It is an arduous task for which a strong, intelligent, tough and very honest personality is essential if justice is to be done. With few exceptions, the judge who has himself ridden in contests up to the standard that he is judging will be a better judge than one who has not, the former being bound to have a better understanding of the problems involved for both horse and rider and of the reasons that may make one horse perform better than another.

In addition to the marks given for each individual movement, four general marks are given at the end of the test attributable to the overall impression with special regard to the basic qualities of good dressage. These general impression marks currently carry a multiplying coefficient of 2, as do certain of the individual movements in the international tests.

The final general-impression marks are allotted under the following headings:

(a) Paces (freedom and regularity).

(b) Impulsion (desire to move forward, elasticity of the steps, suppleness of the back and engagement of the quarters).

(c) Submission (attention and confidence; harmony, lightness and ease of the movements; acceptance of the bridle and lightness of the forehand).

(d) Rider's position and seat; correctness and effect of the aids.

Additional penalties are incurred if the rider forgets the test and/or takes the wrong course in the arena, two marks being deducted by each judge for the first such error, four for the second, and eight for the third. A fourth error of course entails elimination.

APPENDIX A – The Seat

PART 1 – The Seat at the Halt

Almost every rider likes to think that he or she has a good seat on a horse, but it is comparatively rare in this country to see one that will stand up to close scrutiny.

To begin with, a good seat is not something that comes naturally to even the most experienced horsemen who may have ridden all their lives. It has to be acquired by careful study of the requirements followed by a fairly long period of intensive practice. And during that period the student will only achieve success if he is firmly determined never consciously to allow a weakness, however small and in whatever part of his body, to remain unchecked and uncorrected throughout his time in the saddle.

Perfection must be his constant goal until he begins to find that he rides that way by unconscious habit. And even then he must continue to check and recheck for the rest of his riding life.

All this doubtless sounds quite formidable, if not downright forbidding, to beginners, but it is no more so than learning to use the correct and efficient styles and processes for tennis, golf, cricket, skiing, skating or ballroom dancing.

And in all these cases the final acquisition of the correct style is not just a matter of looking pretty or winning the admiration of passers-by. The undeniable fact is that the possession of a good seat is a vital factor in the ability of any rider to get the best out of his horse.

Conversely, a seat that is poor or incorrect, to however small a degree, will proportionately but inevitably interfere with and inhibit the horse's performance.

It follows that, for the sake of his own pride and for the comfort of his horse, there is a powerful obligation on every rider to 'do something about it'. The improvements he will make will pay enormous dividends in his own pleasure and comfort, as in those of his horse. In short, a good seat is good because it is efficient but, being efficient, it is also elegant.

Details of Correct Seat

It is easy enough to sit correctly at the halt and that, after all, is where everything begins, no matter whether you are going thereafter to ride on the flat, over jumps, to hunt, race, play polo or herd stock. Get the basic seat right, and the other variations will follow easily enough. What then is involved in sitting correctly at the halt?

We need to be so positioned that both horse and rider, in partnership, can do the maximum with maximum ease and minimum effort. That necessitates, above all else, that we should be in perfect balance ourselves and that our centre of balance should coincide, whatever happens, with that of the horse.

This position must be one in which the rider can feel relaxed and which he can retain indefinitely without muscular effort or grip. Its details can be found in many books and can be effectively summarised as follows:

(1) Place the seat-bones on the lowest point of the saddle which, to coincide with the centre of balance of the horse, should be about 9in. or 10in. behind the top of the withers.

(2) Put the upper body in balance over the seat-bones (at the bottom of the pelvis) by rocking forward the hip-bones (at the top of the pelvis) so that the pelvis as a whole is so placed that it supports the weight of the torso.

This action will be facilitated if the rider simultaneously lifts his head and neck to ensure that they are well carried above the shoulders. But in practice the rider will immediately notice that the correct positioning of the pelvis directly affects and improves the carriage of the head and shoulders. There will be a proud expansion of the whole front of the rider's body, from bosom to stomach. This is correct and, as will be seen, also essential. The small of the back will be slightly concave. This is exactly the same position as a well-behaved child is expected to adopt when sitting up properly at table.

(3) Allow the legs to hang down naturally, comfortably moulded to the shape of the horse, but with no inward or upward grip. The toes must be held pointing more or less to the front, the heel a little lower than the toes, with the feeling that the weight of the legs flows down into the heel and not into the toes. This feeling is facilitated, when stirrups are used, by placing the stirrup on the ball of the foot.

Allowing the toes to turn out is a bad fault as it tends to clamp and make insensitive the main muscles of the buttocks, thighs and calves and to take the knee away from the horse's side. All these points are detrimental to the efficient use of the legs when they are required to act.

The lower leg should not be drawn back behind the natural hanging position which, because of the weight of the foot, will be just slightly behind the vertical line from the knee. There it will be correctly positioned to operate on the girth which means, in practice, across or just behind the back edge of the girth, and therefore on the most sensitive and flexible area of the horse's body.

If the leg is drawn further back than that it will be in the wrong position to speak effectively to the horse and it will require wasteful muscular effort to keep it there. It must be allowed to hang down, relaxed and easy, without any muscular contraction or effort.

(4) The upper arms should hang vertically down from the shoulders with the elbow-bone lightly brushing the waist or hip-bone. The forearm is then carried so that, when viewed from the side, it points straight towards the bit in the horse's mouth, the reins being merely a prolongation of the forearm.

The wrists are kept straight so that the back of the hand is in line with the forearm, with the thumb uppermost. The hands should be 2–3in. apart.

These positions of arm, wrist and hand are of great importance as they are the positions in which all the muscles of hand and arm are most relaxed and sensitive and therefore capable of being delicate and sympathetic in their dealing with the horse's mouth.

Summary
Such are the vital ingredients of a good seat. They should be practised from the moment the rider gets into the saddle, and maintained even when riding at ease with a long or loose rein or chatting with friends. The question of how to maintain them when in movement, particularly in trot or canter, will be explained in Part 2 of this Appendix. Then every part of the position as here described for the halt will be found to have logical and mechanical functions that, put together, make sitting on the horse in motion relatively easy, comfortable and effective.

PART 2 – The Seat in Motion (Passive)

This section deals with the negative aspect of ensuring that our presence in the saddle does not cause positive discomfort or inconvenience to the horse, thereby making his work more difficult and more tiring than it need be.

If the rider fails in this respect he will gradually but assuredly spoil the horse because the discomfort he will cause will make it virtually impossible for the animal to operate to the best of its ability. Work will consequently deteriorate.

The rider's problem begins the moment the horse moves forward into a walk and is further accentuated by the trot and the canter. The principles are the same, however, at all paces.

In each case, the rider has to be able to maintain his exact balance over the centre of balance of the horse without gripping to hold himself in place. That might not be too difficult if the horse moved smoothly along the ground like a bicycle, but of course he does not.

In all equine movement there is a degree of upward as well as forward thrust, both being more or less spasmodic and both having to be absorbed and followed, smoothly and harmoniously, so as not to disturb the rider's, and consequently also the horse's, balance. More precisely, this has to be done without any of that bumping in the saddle which sooner or later causes discomfort and even injury to both parties; which looks unsightly; and which

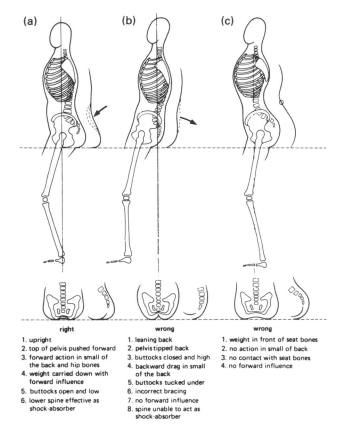

(a)   (b)   (c)

right	wrong	wrong
1. upright	1. leaning back	1. weight in front of seat bones
2. top of pelvis pushed forward	2. pelvis tipped back	2. no action in small of back
3. forward action in small of the back and hip bones	3. buttocks closed and high	3. no contact with seat bones
4. weight carried down with forward influence	4. backward drag in small of the back	4. no forward influence
5. buttocks open and low	5. buttocks tucked under	
6. lower spine effective as shock-absorber	6. incorrect bracing	
	7. no forward influence	
	8. spine unable to act as shock-absorber	

Fig. 36   *The mechanics and influence of the seat.*

eventually destroys the horse's paces.

To overcome these problems requires a little under-standing of simple mechanics, and some practice. If the understanding is not there, the practice seldom produces a successful development from that basic seat at the halt. So we must take a look at the mechanics.

Perhaps the simplest way to grasp the mechanical problem is to imagine a broomstick balanced vertically on a diving-board. If the diving-board is then activated, the broomstick will bounce on the board, rising higher in the air than the board at its highest point, and consequently coming down again out of timing and striking the board just after it has started its next upward stroke. There will be a continuous series of very unrhythmic bumps.

If, on the other hand, the end of a short piece of rope is placed on the board, with the other end being held up aloft to allow just a slight bulge at the lower end, the rope will remain quietly and snugly on the board without loss of contact when the latter is activated.

Now the rider's pelvis, on which he sits, has no flexibility but his spine, which is attached to the pelvis, has. It is the rider's prime task to ensure that his spine operates like the rope on the diving-board and not like the broomstick.

It is almost, if not quite, as simple as that.

The difference between the horse and the diving-board is that the former moves forward as well as up and down. But fortunately our anatomy is such that it is able to deal simultaneously with the two forms of movement. It will do this for us almost automatically, provided only that we set up the machine in the proper manner (as already described in Part 1 of this Appendix) with, in particular, the top of the pelvis or hip-bone tipped forward into its balanced position above the seat-bones.

This position, the key to all that follows, results in a pronounced forward bulge in the lower end of the spinal column where, in its strongest and most flexible part, it lies within the pelvis itself.

From that basic position the spine can and will do two things, the combination of which will produce the still, quiet seat in the saddle that we all strive to acquire but which eludes so many riders. These two functions are:

First, the spine will absorb the upward thrust of the

horse, and the subsequent bump as the rider comes down in the saddle, because the forward bulge at the lower end will act as a shock-absorber by flexing momentarily even further forward under the two stresses, thereby shortening the overall distance between the seat-bones and the shoulders. The pelvis, being attached to the spine, will be rocked further forward by the increased flexion of the latter.

The result of this shock-absorbing action is that the rider will not be thrown up into the air like the broomstick; the seat-bones will remain in the saddle; the shoulders, and therefore the hands, will remain more or less still; and there should be no nodding of the head.

As the saddle then falls away again, the flexed spine will tend to straighten and lengthen itself; the pelvis will be rocked back to its original position; and the seat-bones will stay in the saddle as it falls. Conversely, if the lower spine does not flex in this manner, with every stride, then the opposite of all these desirable things will occur.

The flexion, and reflexion of the spine which is clearly visible to the spectator, will and must be constant. It is recognised in a slight, clear but supple concavity of the small of the back. This is of great importance because of the position into which it places the spine.

Second, the spine will, by flexing forward, ensure that the gravitational weight of the torso is carried diagonally downward-and-forward, instead of just vertically downward, enabling the rider, with little conscious effort, to follow the forward movement of the horse, as well as remaining close to the saddle.

Following the movement is the conventional phrase, though it may be preferable to refer to going with, or accompanying, the movement. The rider should not be following from behind; he is not dragged along by the horse; he should accompany the movement easily and simultaneously as a good dancing partner does.

We have seen that the flexion of the lower spine and the rocking of the pelvis over the seat-bones are not only vitally important but are linked together and co-ordinated by the junction of the one to the other. The rider will not be able to feel the flexing in his spine, but he will be quite conscious of the rocking of his pelvis and he can thus, to a considerable extent, judge for himself whether or not the double action is occurring as it should.

He may also find it useful when first practising the action to initiate it, or cause it to happen, by consciously and deliberately pushing forward his hip-bones (the top of the pelvis) with each stride, thus creating the extra forward flexion of the spine that immediately becomes his shock absorber.

The pushing forward of the hip-bones is done by bracing the muscles of the loins or lumbar region. It is very important when bracing the back in this way to ensure that the full weight of the rider remains firmly on the seat-bones and that the shoulders do not get in front of the vertical line through them. It is the latter fault that produces the undesirable hollow-back in which the rider is no longer truly sitting on the seat-bones but is perching on his thighs.

If the pelvis is not constantly pressed forward, or is allowed to tip backwards, the spine, as can be seen in the diagram, loses most of its bulge; becomes much straighter; begins to act more like the broomstick than the rope; and the rider bumps.

It will not be necessary for the rider to make any conscious muscular effort to rock the pelvis back to its original position, ready for the next move forward. He only has to cease the forward bracing of the loins and the rest will happen of its own accord, brought about by the related inter-action of his weight and the thrust and fall of the horse.

A positive withdrawal of the hip-bones would require a

strong action of the muscles of the stomach, but this would be unnecessarily tiring, unsightly, difficult to co-ordinate with the bracing, and detrimental to the harmony of the combined horse/rider movement.

We have so far dealt with the actions of the lumbar spine and pelvis as required solely for the relatively passive business of merely sitting still, whether stationary or in motion, in a manner that is easy and comfortable for the horse and the rider.

If the rider has such a seat, the horse will not be unduly inconvenienced and will be capable of giving his best. But he will not necessarily do so unless the rider can also use his seat, when required, in a more positive and demanding manner. That aspect of the seat will be dealt with in the third section of this Appendix.

PART 3 – The Seat in Motion (Positive)

We have examined the problems that confront the rider in learning to sit still in the saddle in a balanced and relaxed manner that will avoid any discomfort or undue inconvenience to his horse, or to himself. Neither party will get unnecessarily tired and the horse will function happily and efficiently.

All that, however essential as a first step to acquiring a good seat, represents only a relatively passive stage in which the rider asks no serious questions but merely accommodates himself to the horse's movement.

He will probably look quite elegant, but he will not yet be an efficient and effective horseman. He has still to learn how to make major and positive demands without, in doing so, inconveniencing the horse. The seat should always be still and supple; on occasion it should be still, supple, positive and powerful. The latter activity is naturally much more difficult than the former.

At this stage the rider is bound to make increasing use of the legs as well as the pelvis, to the extent that neither can function to full effect without the other. Legs and pelvis become one and indivisible, though either can be predominant over the other, depending on the circumstances of the moment and the degree of finesse and harmony achieved by rider and horse.

We have, nevertheless, to acknowledge one important distinction. That part of the rider that sits in the saddle cannot by itself create any significant activity from the horse, against its will. For that, the seat, or pelvis, has to be supported by a complementary action of the legs.

On the other hand the legs can, if only rather crudely, cause the horse to move forward or sideways without noticeable assistance from the seat itself. In brief, it is normally the job of the rider's legs to create activity, and the job of the seat to influence, encourage or modify the resulting action.

There are strong limitations to what the seat can do by itself, but nevertheless the part it plays is vital to the end result. Because it has virtually no direct mechanical power to create movement, its effect can be regarded as largely psychological, although none the less important for that.

But whatever the source of its strength, its effect is undeniable and invaluable, provided it is used correctly. That is done by merely intensifying the muscularity of the same pelvic action that we have seen to be an integral part of good but passive sitting.

For good, passive sitting we had to rock the top of the pelvis forward a little with each step so as to ensure that the lower spine would flex forward and absorb the normal but inevitable tendency to bump. That same action also carried us forward so that we followed, or accompanied, the movement.

To initiate that pelvic action we had lightly to use, or brace, the muscles of our loins or small of the back. If now, when we wish to exert a more positive influence, we brace those same muscles more strongly, we shall:

(a) Make the shock absorber stronger and more powerful;

(b) Somewhat reduce the degree of supple, forward flexion of the spine;

(c) Increase the influence of the seat-bones on the saddle and therefore also on the horse's back muscles;

(d) Cause the spring-like shape of the lumbar spine,

acting in a forward and downward direction, to *draw* forward the seat-bones on the saddle, thus exerting a distinct forward-urging influence on the horse.

It cannot be too strongly stressed that the seat-bones are *drawn* forward, and not pushed forward by a backward-tilted pelvis. The latter action is sometimes recommended in contemporary equestrian literature, but it can only be done by more or less straightening the natural curve of the lumbar spine, thereby destroying the vital shock-absorber as well as the rider's ability to swing forward *with the movement*.

It also disturbs the natural balance of the rider by placing his weight too far back, and against the movement. It constitutes a fallacious and even disastrous conception of forward-urging on 'driving' aids.

It must be understood that, when the pelvis draw is carried out correctly, the seat-bones do not actually shift their position on the saddle. Perhaps they will move fractionally over the skin that covers them, but the skin certainly does not move at all – there is no forward and backward sliding action in the saddle that would eventually wear out the breeches and probably also the saddle.

The required forward-urging effect of the seat when used in this manner is achieved solely by the direction of the rider's weight on his seat-bones aided by the bracing of the lumbar muscles as, for example, when the end of one thumb is drawn forward on the loose skin on the back of the other hand, but without actually moving on that skin. That, with the resulting psychological influence, is all the sometimes vaunted 'driving aid of the seat' can do.

Finally, it should be appreciated that even that relatively mild form of seat-aid should not be used unless and until the muscles of the horse's back have been well developed and are, at that moment, swinging well.

To use that degree of muscle pressure on a back that is

either weak or not swinging actively would be to run a very real risk of flattening the horse even more than he already was. It will certainly not induce the back to swing and will probably cause the horse to withdraw it, thus spoiling his performance and his paces.

APPENDIX B – The Half-halt

An eminent figure in international dressage was once asked what he thought was the chief cause of Great Britain's poor performance in the dressage discipline. He replied without hesitation and in three words: 'No half-halts'. They are, he added, the quintessence of dressage. In varying forms that opinion has been repeated over and over again whenever the same problem has been discussed by competent critics outside this country. It would therefore seem that unless we are prepared to claim to be the only nation in step, we have little option but to take the accusation seriously.

How did this situation arise? It came about because, in the formative years of British dressage, say the fifteen years between 1950 and 1965, when a whole new tradition and set of teaching formulae had to be forged from scratch, there were few if any professional teachers who appreciated the importance of this subtlety and its all-pervading role in dressage. Some of those who did have some knowledge of it also knew that the half-halt was difficult to assimilate, and the word was put around that we could get on well enough if we ignored the tiresome thing. So the majority of the first generation of dressage riders were not encouraged to study the subject and, since dressage in any form was supposed in those days to be well beyond the scope of the Pony Club, the second generation grew up in total ignorance of it. Once established, old habits are hard to change.

Another complicating factor is that even today's instructors who understand the matter very well hardly

ever give the half-halts more than a casual mention. They
are seldom heard actually teaching or explaining the
subject. They appear either to take it for granted that
everyone knows and understands, or to believe that the
subject is above the heads of most of their pupils. So one
way or another, the ignorance of those early years has to a
considerable extent been perpetuated.

What is the purpose of the half-halt and why is it essential?
In the simplest terms, it is a call for attention that is used
to regain or re-establish balance, impulsion and collection
or any one of those qualities. It is essential because the
horse, being mainly an unthinking athlete, cannot be
relied on to maintain its peak output all the time without
continual encouragement and assistance from its rider.
Yet dressage demands the utmost diligence and effort if it
is to be of real aesthetic or physical value, and the almost
continuous refreshing stimulation by the rider, through
the use of half-halts, becomes a *sine qua non*.

How often are half-halts brought into play? As often as
possible? More often than can be counted? In an almost
continuous succession? A dozen or so times in the course
of one circuit of a large arena? The answer to the main
question will lie somewhere among those alternatives, all
of which may be valid. In practice, the frequency will
increase with the degree of finesse of the rider and the
degree of suppleness and obedience that he has built into
the training of his horse.

Half-halts are an acquired art and habit for both
parties, and a lot of hard work and study goes into their
acquisition. They are easy only when they become
second nature, not least because the achievement of each
and every one puts a considerable strain on the musculature of both horse and rider and are tiring to both.

*What actually happens in a half-halt, and how is it
executed?* All the important or famous books on dressage
give some sort of definition, though many fall somewhat

short of making everything as clear as daylight for the inexperienced student. The Official Rules, for example, say that it is 'a hardly visible, almost simultaneous, coordinated action of the seat, legs and hand . . .'. However difficult it may be to improve on that statement, it could be argued that it is more effective in saying what a half-halt should not be than in explaining precisely what the rider has to do, and in what sequence, and when. Richard Wätjen, on the other hand, says categorically that the aids of seat and hand should be simultaneous, so clearly there is room for careful thought and study.

The essential components of a half-halt are always the same, consisting of a forward urge by the loins, seat and legs, complemented by a compressing action of the fingers of one or both hands, the latter strong enough to prevent the horse from increasing speed as the result of the former. The compressing action of the hand will vary considerably in degree according to the extent to which the rider wishes, if at all, to reduce speed. Every rider has to discover for himself the infinitely varying niceties of these aids, though there is one universal and golden rule to remember: never hang on to or prolong the rein aid if it is met by resistance from the horse. The compression, whether successful or not, must be released almost immediately so that it will not, by its severity, cause the horse to resent and stiffen against it.

What the rider hopes to achieve and to feel happening under him, as the direct result of these aids, is an immediate increase in the longitudinal suppleness and submission of his horse's back, neck and poll. The increased engagement of the quarters and the complementary restraint at the front will, or should, cause the back to come up to him in a soft and rounded manner which in turn will cause the neck to arch and the poll and mouth to soften and submit. It can be, and should be, a beautiful feeling.

It is, however, useless to expect these things to happen as a matter of course, with any horse at any time without regard to its training and education. The half-halt has to be worked up and developed gradually, like any other movement or exercise, and therein lies the difficulty. It is hopeless to try to compress the front end of a stiff horse while urging him on by the seat. He will not understand and will either go faster or become even stiffer. The horse in those circumstances can be likened to a handful of putty with which a glazier intends to insert a new pane of glass in a window. The putty has first to be worked and kneaded until it is warm and soft right through, before it can be applied effectively to the window frame. Similarly the horse must have reached a degree of suppleness through the previous training processes, and must have acquired a degree of mental submission to leg and rein aids, before he can be expected to understand and obey the somewhat contradictory aids of the half-halt. In other words, the young horse has to be loosened, suppled and educated to the aids before work on half-halts can usefully be commenced in the context of the overall training programme. And by the same token, every horse needs to be loosened and suppled every day before the half-halts can be, as they should be, given their daily polish-up, in the same way that a pianist will run over a few scales each day, after first warming his hands, before beginning work on some major piece of music.

A further point to remember is that the horse must be on the bit in the fullest sense of the phrase before he can be expected to comply with a half-halt. It is physically impossible, for example, for a horse that is above the bit to react to the aids in the manner described above. From an above-the-bit posture we cannot obtain that cycle of aids between reins, seat and hindlegs that is the essence of all good dressage and of the half-halt in particular, and which results in the hindlegs being drawn a little further under the mass by the restraint imposed on the front end by the reins. It can hardly be repeated too often that this effect can never come about unless the back of the horse is longitudinally supple. Without that prerequisite, the hindlegs cannot come forward. The smallest tendency of the horse to flatten or hollow his back as the result of rein action will destroy any prospect of an effective half-halt.

It is not practical to lay down a hard and fast rule as to precisely how every horse should be worked every day but, with regard to the daily revision of the half-halt effect – something that should be as regular as brushing the hair when getting out of bed in the morning – it is difficult to improve on the practice and recommendation of the most famous amateur trainer of our time, Dr Reiner Klimke. After first loosening his horse with some free-going and low work in trot and canter, Dr Klimke will begin to work in a more collected manner and then run through the half-halt drill in its simplest and most basic form. Moving on a circle to make it easier, he will in turn revise the trot-walk-trot transitions, the canter-trot-canter transitions and finally, if the horse has reached that stage of training, the canter-walk-canter. When the horse has been 'won' in body and mind in these basic forms, always remaining sufficiently deep and on the bit in every upward and downward transition, the stage will be set for any form of work in which half-halts will be used without involving a transition from one gait to another. The same physical response through the horse will occur, but the gait will remain unchanged unless or until specific aids are given to change the gait. Gradually, as time goes on, the aids will more and more lightly and accurately produce the delightful and beautiful sensation of come-uppance which we tried to describe in an earlier paragraph.

Index